S0-CWU-711

The Victor KNOW & BELIEVE Series

This book is part of The Victor KNOW & BELIEVE Series, an eight-volume library of the major doctrines of the Bible all of which are written in a clear, down-to-earth style. Other books in the series are:

The Bible: Breathed from God (Bibliology), Robert L. Saucy, Th.D.

The Church: God's People (Ecclesiology), Bruce L. Shelley, Ph.D.

The Future Explored (Eschatology), Timothy P. Weber, Ph.D.

The Holy Spirit: Comforter, Teacher, Guide (Pneumatology), Fred P. Thompson, S.T.D.

The Living God (Theology), Robert D. Culver, Th.D.

Jesus Christ: The God-Man (Christology), Bruce A. Demarest, Ph.D.

Man: Ruined and Restored (Anthropology), Leslie B. Flynn, B.D., M.A.

Salvation: God's Amazing Plan (Soteriology), Millard J. Erickson, Ph.D.

Editor of the Series is Bruce L. Shelley, Ph.D., professor of Church History, Conservative Baptist Theological Seminary, Denver, Colorado.

VICTOR Know and Believe SERIES

The
Future
Explored

Timothy P. Weber

Edited by Bruce L. Shelley

This book is designed for your personal reading
pleasure and profit. It is also designed for group
study. A leader's guide with helps and hints for
teachers and with visual aids (Victor Multiuse Trans-
parency Masters) is available from your local bookstore or from the publisher at $2.25.

VICTOR BOOKS

a division of SP Publications, Inc., Wheaton, Illinois
Offices also in Fullerton, California • Whitby, Ontario, Canada • London, England

Unless otherwise noted, all Scripture quotations are from the *New International Version: New Testament* (NIV), © 1973, The New York Bible Society International. Other quotations are from the King James Version (KJV), and *The New American Standard Bible* (*NASB*), © 1960, 1962, 1963, 1968, 1971, 1972, 1973, The Lockman Foundation, La Habra, Calif. All quotations used by permission.

Library of Congress Catalog Card Number: 77-015703
ISBN: 0-88207-763-5

© 1978 by SP Publications, Inc. All rights reserved
Printed in the United States of America

VICTOR BOOKS
a division of SP Publications, Inc.
P.O. Box 1825 ● Wheaton, Illinois 60187

Contents

Preface

Eschatology is a difficult subject because evangelicals who agree on nearly everything else often can't seem to get together on the details of prophetic interpretation.

I have sincerely tried to be fair to the major positions held by premillennialists today. Where evangelicals disagree, I have attempted to explain why, careful to present the best arguments on both sides. Instead of trying to prove one point of view over another, I have chosen to stress those things which all premillennialists can agree on: the blessed hope of Christ's return, His ultimate victory over sin, death, Satan, and the forces of evil, and the important place which the people of God will share in the victory. In addition, I have endeavored to point out some of the practical consequences these biblical truths should make in our daily lives.

Since this is my first book, special thanks are in order. First, I'd like to express my appreciation to Dr. Bruce Shelley, the editor of this series and my colleague in church history at Conservative Baptist Theological Seminary in Denver, and to Victor Books. Though they offered valuable and helpful assistance along the way, any major deficiencies in the finished product are mine alone.

Second, and most of all, I wish to thank my wife, Linda, who will never really know how much she contributes to what I do. Not only did she willingly submit to countless interruptions in order to listen to ideas and unfinished paragraphs, but she consistently tried to get me to set—and then keep—writing schedules. For that reason alone, this is her book too.

Finally, I want to dedicate this book to my parents, Jack and Ruth Weber of Sierra Madre, California, whose Christian home, personal examples, and inexhaustible supply of love and support have been among the most important and enduring things in my life.

Introduction

Signs of evangelical vitality are all around us. Prominent personalities from politics, sports and entertainment have recently "come out" for Christ. Publication houses report record sales of evangelical titles. Large conventions of evangelical believers catch the eye of the national wire services and the major magazines. The public is discovering the meaning of "born again."

This rather sudden exposure in the secular press has a happy side and a sad side. The happy side is the opportunity for millions of Americans to encounter the Gospel of Jesus Christ. For a half-century biblical Christianity has received mostly scorn from the spokesmen of American culture—movies, newspapers, novels and television. The public was so busy laughing at the Gospel that it couldn't listen to it. Today, some are listening.

The sad side of this exposure is the evident weakness of "born again" religion. The major polls reveal that it is largely experience-centered, and almost any weird brush with mystery seems to do.

Biblical Christianity has an experiential element, but it is linked with doctrine and Body. It is what we think and to what we belong as well as what we experience.

That is where this book and others in the Victor Know and Believe Series comes in. These eight books, designed for personal or group studies, aim at adding truth to testimony. As evangelicals, we should not only speak up in American society; may we say something when we do.

Bruce L. Shelley
Editor

1

Second Coming Confusion

Society at large has become aware of the growing popularity of eschatology, thanks to a number of best-selling books on the subject. Hal Lindsey's *The Late Great Planet Earth* has sold over 12 million copies since 1970 and can be found in drugstores and supermarkets right alongside diet books, gothic romances, detective stories, and westerns. The resurgence of the interest in prophetic themes is one of the most significant developments in American religion since the Second World War.

What then is *eschatology?* The term comes from two Greek words: *eschaton,* meaning "last or end," and *logos* meaning "word, thought, or reason." Strictly speaking, then, eschatology refers to what we think or say about the end of the world. That sounds easy enough, but it isn't. Despite its popularity and apparent simplicity, eschatology is a difficult business.

Anyone who writes a book on eschatology knows that he cannot possibly please everybody. Too many different people expect too many different things. Some readers want those who write books on prophetic themes to be daring and speculative; others want them to be conservative and noncommittal. Some evangelicals expect to be provided with elaborate charts of future events, educated guesses on how close we are to the

Second Coming, and frequent guarantees that the author's interpretations are the only ones possible. Yet many other evangelicals are tired of the arguments about the end times and view them as theological hairsplitting over matters that will be settled one day by the Lord's return. Those who dare write books on eschatology, therefore, are bound to disappoint large segments of evangelicals, no matter what they write!

Another Book?

Why *another* book on eschatology? That's a good question. There seem to be too many on the market as it is! Here's an even better question: Why is a *church historian* writing another book on eschatology?

Whenever the evangelical church gives so much attention to one particular part of biblical truth, it always runs the risk of becoming lopsided, which can actually distort the doctrine's proper place in the overall biblical scheme of things. We can detect such a tendency today. Growing numbers of believers are beginning to realize that we have not always taken a balanced biblical approach to the study of eschatology.

We have become so consumed with the *what, when,* and *how* questions concerning the second coming of Jesus Christ that we have neglected the *why's* and the *so what's.* To put it another way, often we forget to ask two essential questions when we approach Bible study: (1) What does the Bible actually teach (the who, what, when, and how questions)? and (2) What difference should this teaching make in our daily living (the why and so what questions)? If we are not concerned with both sets of questions, then we run the risk of becoming out of balance with the proper biblical view.

So Many Views

Before we can answer these questions, however, we have to get our bearings. Most Christians have quite definite ideas about eschatology without realizing how difficult the issues are or how many views exist. Most of us are exposed to one or two eschatological points of view during our lifetimes and never come in contact with the many different options which have existed in Christian history. Most of us assume that what we believe is what the church has always believed. Whereas that assumption may hold true about a lot of things, it is not true about eschatology.

Here are four basic questions about the end times and a few of the different answers that Christians have given to them over the centuries:

1. *Will there be a literal, earthly millennium?* Some Christians have said yes to a thousand-year reign of Christ on earth and others no. Such notable believers as Augustine, Martin Luther, John Calvin, and John Wesley claimed that biblical passages on the Millennium should be taken figuratively. They and their followers (who include most of today's Lutherans, Presbyterians, Reformed, and Methodists) believe that "the Millennium" refers to the reign of Christ in individual hearts (which begins at conversion) or the reign of Christ in the world through the church (which began at Pentecost). This position is the *amillennial* viewpoint, which literally means "no millennium."

Many other believers throughout church history have been equally convinced that all references to the Millennium in the Scriptures should be taken literally and that we can expect the establishment of an earthly millennial kingdom. These Christians are called *millennialists.*

2. *What is the relationship between the Millennium and the second coming of Christ?* Christian millennialists have given two basic answers. *Postmillennialists* believe that Christ will return *after* the Millennium has been established through the Spirit-empowered evangelistic and missionary activity of the church. *Premillennialists,* on the other hand, believe that Christ will return *before* the Millennium in order to set it up through His majesty and power.

3. *What should be our basic approach to the prophecies of the "last days"?* Premillennialists have been traditionally divided in two groups on this question. *Historicists* (who made

up most of the premillennialists before 1850) argue that the "last days" refer to the entire Church Age. They, therefore, interpret prophecies of the end as though they intended to provide a picture of the entire sweep of church history. The rise of Antichrist, the Tribulation, and the prophecies concerning the "vials" in the Book of Revelation, for example, have already been fulfilled in church history, according to the historicists.

Futurists, however, view the "last days" as the brief period immediately before the Lord's return. They expect all end-time prophecies to be fulfilled in a short time just before the Second Coming. In other words, historicist premillennialists look backward into history for the fulfillment of prophecy, while futurists look forward into the future.

4. *When will the Rapture occur in relation to the Tribulation?* It is safe to say that most American evangelicals who trace their roots back to fundamentalism are futurist premillennialists. They believe that Christ will actually set up an earthly millennium and that prophecies of the last days are yet to be fulfilled. But there the agreement often ends. Historically, futurist premillennialists have disagreed on when the "rapture" of the church will take place. "Rapture" is the term we use to designate the sudden change and departure of living believers from this world when the Lord Jesus comes again.

Strangely enough, during most of church history, premillennialists have not been too concerned about the timing of the Rapture. Sometimes they ignored the question completely, and at other times their teaching was not always clear. For example, certain early church fathers taught an imminent return of Christ, but because they were undergoing severe persecution at the hands of the Romans, they also believed that they were already in the Tribulation.

Though historians are still sifting through the evidence, it appears that there was no major disagreement among premillennialists on this issue until the early nineteenth century. Up to that time historicist and futurist premillennialists alike seemed to teach that the church will be raptured at the end of the tribulation period. This view is called *posttribulationism*. Then during the late 1820s, John Nelson Darby, a gifted Bible teacher and one of the early leaders of the Plymouth Brethren in Great Britain, began to teach that the rapture of the church would occur before the Tribulation ever got under way. Darby's teaching about a *pretribulation rapture of the church* was only part of an entire approach to biblical interpretation called "dispensationalism," after his division of history into various "dispensations," or eras.

When Darby began teaching the pretribulation rapture, he met with considerable opposition from many believers, including some of his fellow Plymouth Brethren. Despite the charges of novelty which were levelled against him, Darby was convinced that God had given him new light on a doctrine which had been long misunderstood. He said that his rapture doctrine had grown out of a new insight into the nature of the church in its relation to Israel. According to Darby, God has two completely separate plans operating in history: one for an earthly people (Israel) and another for a heavenly people (the church). "To rightly divide the word of truth," one must keep the two completely apart. Keeping this principle foremost in his mind, Darby developed a rule of thumb for biblical interpretation: all prophecies which apply to earthly events belong to Israel (God's earthly people) and all those which have to do with heaven belong to the church (God's heavenly people). Thus to apply earthly prophecies to God's heavenly people is to commit the most serious mistake in biblical interpretation. So passages which speak of the saints going through the Tribulation (Matthew 24 or Revelation 7 or 14), *must* be interpreted as referring to Israel and not the church.

Darby's teaching quickly spread to this country and made dramatic inroads into American evangelicalism. By 1900, pretribulationism was being taught by some of American evangelicalism's most gifted and respected leaders and came to predominate in Bible and prophetic conferences and Bible institutes. Though *posttribulationism* (the belief that Christ will return to rapture the church after the Tribulation) was the older clearly taught position, it had been outstripped by dispensational pretribulationism by the 1920s.

Just to make things more confusing than they already are, there are premillennialists who hold a *midtribulation* position, teaching that the church will be raptured *halfway* through the period, after the Antichrist is revealed but before God pours out His wrath on the earth.

To bring the whole discussion into sharper focus, see the chart of the various eschatological positions held in the church over the years on page 15.

Most Christians are honestly disturbed by such divisions in the body of Christ. Such disagreements have often led to fierce battles between Christians. Conflicts over eschatology have split churches and broken friendships. In some places, a person's Christian orthodoxy or even his personal faith is judged by whether he is an "amill," a "premill," a "pretrib," or a "posttrib!"

Certainly there is nothing new about disagreements in the Christian church. Just look around your own community. Some evangelical churches baptize infants, while others baptize only believers. Some sprinkle, others immerse. Some are congregational in their church government, while others are organized along presbyterian or episcopal lines. Most Christians use musical instruments in their worship services, but some refuse on the grounds that they were not used in the New Testament. While evangelicals agree on the fundamentals of the faith, they often disagree on many secondary matters.

Possibly we should view the disagreements over eschatology in this light, but at the same time recognize that there are some serious issues at stake. For example, how can born-again Christians who believe in the inspiration and authority of the Bible not agree on what it says? Or how can people who sincerely seek the Spirit's guidance in such matters come to opposite conclusions? How is the average Christian going to decide between these different views?

Views of Christian Eschatology

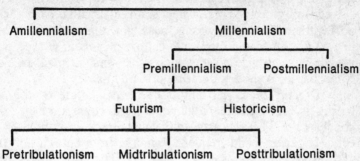

Amillennialism   Millennialism

Premillennialism   Postmillennialism

Futurism   Historicism

Pretribulationism   Midtribulationism   Posttribulationism

How to Decide

Most of us use one or more of the following methods in trying to decide between different Christian points of view.

1. *Taking Spiritual Temperatures.* Some people try to determine the truthfulness of someone's beliefs by examining how he lives. If someone is living a consistent Christian life, separated from the world, according to certain Christians, his beliefs are probably correct. We have all seen how certain godly people carry an awful lot of weight in Bible studies or church business meetings. For better or worse, their theological opinions attain almost instant respectability because of the kind of lives they lead.

This method of deciding between rival points of view can be called "taking spiritual temperatures." According to this approach, the truth of a doctrine is determined not by *what* it is as much as by *who* believes it. Someone using this method must ask himself, "Who is more godly, Dr. Jones or Dr. Smith? Who is living more consistently according to biblical principles, the pretribs or the posttribs?"

Fortunately, most people see the foolishness of this whole approach. First, it is almost impossible to get a reliable reading in such matters and to generalize about whole groups of people. Second, in evangelical Christianity, doctrine is determined by Scripture, not by who happens to hold it.

Anyone who takes the time can discover that there are godly, Spirit-filled believers on all sides of these issues. We are correct in expecting correct beliefs and Christlike behavior to go together, but we're wrong to assume that one necessarily proves the other. Godly people can be mistaken; wicked people can have all the right theological answers. Remember, even Satan has an orthodox doctrine of God (James 2:19).

2. *Digging In.* Other ambitious Christians are determined to dig in, read all the arguments, and come to their own conclusions. These hearty souls make regular purchases at Bible bookstores and frequently emerge from church libraries with armfuls of books on eschatology. They are walking encyclopedias who become experts in an area which causes many PhDs to tear their hair and climb the walls. They can instantly recite the various views of Drs. X, Y, and Z with great precision and more often than not, their personal libraries rival the holdings on eschatology in many Bible institutes.

These people deserve our admiration, but they are not altogether a special breed. Almost any person who takes the time can make eschatology a "hobby," gain tremendous insight into the various positions, and come to his own conclusions.

3. *Relying on the Experts.* Most of us, however, do not want to make eschatology our life's work. Other pressures are too great, the arguments too confusing. We'd rather leave the whole business to some trusted Bible teacher, pastor, or seminary professor who has spent years studying the subject and ought to know what he is talking about. We'll take his word for it.

This method makes a lot of sense for most of us. After all, we live in an age of experts. Why not rely on the opinions of an expert in eschatology in the same way we rely on the opinions of our mechanic, furnace inspector, or medical doctor?

Even though most of us feel compelled to rely on the work of others, that really doesn't solve the problem. That's just putting the responsibility on someone else. To make matters worse—which expert do we choose when *they* can't agree among themselves? There are experts on both sides of every issue! What do we do then—count the number of academic degrees?

By this time, most of us can understand why some Christians want to forget the whole thing. Isn't there any way to resolve these differences or learn to live together?

Naturally, there is always the chance that as believers continue studying the Word of God, there will be a meeting of the minds. That kind of thing has happened before, and it might happen again. But even if the church of Christ does not attain perfect agreement on these matters, it agrees on far more than it disagrees—even when it comes to eschatology. All evangelicals, no matter what they think about the timing of the Rapture or what Christians will be doing in the Millennium, can honestly confess that Jesus Christ is personally, visibly, and powerfully going to return to rapture the church, raise the dead, break once and for all the powers of darkness, and bring the Father's redemptive purposes to a fitting and final conclusion. This has always been the historic doctrine of the church, and all Christians, no matter what their particular eschatological view, can affirm it without reservation.

Now that we have gotten our bearings—and hopefully obtained a certain degree of humility which will not permit us to consign those who don't agree with us on eschatology to the outer darkness—let's begin our study of what the Bible actually teaches about the end of the world. After what we have just seen, don't be surprised if you won't be able to agree with everything I'm about to say. Some people will think I've gone too far, others not far enough. But I will try to be as fair as possible and constantly affirm what all evangelicals can agree on.

2

What in the World Is God Doing?

People today are fascinated by the future. Bookstore shelves bulge with do-it-yourself horoscope guides. Department stores and occult shops are selling tarot cards and Ouija boards at a record pace. Professional astrologers have never had so many paying customers. Even people who question the validity of astrology often turn, out of curiosity, to the horoscopes in the morning paper. As strange as it may seem in this day of science and technology, increasing numbers of educated and otherwise sophisticated people are consulting mediums, attending seances, and seeking the services of palm readers and crystal ball gazers.

Astrology addicts and dabblers in the occult are not the only people whose daily lives are calculated by their concerns and beliefs about the future. Though we often fail to recognize it, most of us make important decisions with the future in mind. How we think of tomorrow determines to a large degree what we do today.

Calculating the Present in Light of the Future

Take, for example, business executives. They make many of their crucial decisions on the basis of what they think will happen in the future. Their carefully calculated projections about the stock market will determine whether they stand pat, invest more capital, or sell what stocks they already own. Every year millions of dollars are made and lost by people who have guessed correctly or incorrectly about the whims and wishes of the consuming public. Whether or not someone invests in property, buys municipal bonds, takes a chance on long-term mutual funds, expands or cuts back production, or plays it safe by depositing money in a guaranteed high interest account will be decided to a great extent by what he thinks the future economy will be like.

College students also make present decisions in light of future expectations. Most students choose their course of study on the basis of where they think the jobs will be by the time they graduate. Not many years ago, experts predicted severe shortages in the teaching and engineering professions, so thousands of young people majored in education and engineering. But by the early 1970s, the job opportunities in these areas suddenly dried up. As a result, thousands of people with training in these fields could not find jobs—all because they had accepted an erroneous idea about the future.

Consequently, students today are more careful about selecting college majors. Placement courselors report that the most prevalent question asked on campuses is, "If I take this course of study, what will I be able to do with it when I get out?"

Similarly, in the last few years most of us have become aware of the great ecological disasters which lie in the future if we don't take present action. Dismal reports from geologists and petroleum engineers prompted President Jimmy Carter to propose a stiff energy program in 1977 to preserve fuel reserves and forestall a major catastrophe in the years ahead. Fears about the future have already led some people to purchase more gas-efficient automobiles and turn their thermostats down in the winter.

The Larger Question
Clearly, then, what we do now is determined to a significant degree by what we think will happen later. In much the same

way, societies and nations frequently take shape and make important decisions on the basis of a much larger question than the future state of the economy or the condition of the job market five or ten years from now. In many ways the most basic question of them all is, where is the human race headed, or where is history going?

Many people are too busy making a living for themselves and their families to be concerned about such a "philosophical" matter as mankind's destiny. But when people do take the time to come up with some kind of answer, their lives will reflect it in a variety of ways.

One common view of history is *cyclical*, in which the course of human events is viewed as part of an endless, recurring cycle in which nothing ever really changes. Repetition is the rule, not the exception. Try as we might, there is nothing we can do to change things one way or the other. In many traditional Eastern cultures, this cyclical view has combined with certain religious ideas to make human progress almost impossible. In India, for example, the Hindu concept of *karma* holds that a person's present condition in life is the result of the good or bad which he committed in a previous existence. His status in a future life, in turn, will be determined by how well he accepts his present condition. Consequently, even those people who are terribly oppressed or underprivileged are often very reluctant to try to improve or change their condition for fear they will be in even worse shape the next time around. In this case, an individual's view of the future holds him in bondage in the present.

Another view of history is *linear*, in which history has a beginning, a middle, and an end. History is thought to be going somewhere, and even has some meaning and order, though most people can't seem to agree on what the meaning and order are. Usually people who hold this view believe in some kind of progress. In the end, they believe, historical development is always upward. Though there may be ups and downs and advances and retreats along the way, over the long run things will get better. People with this perspective have always felt freer to try to change things; in fact, one might even argue, the linear view of history is largely responsible for the development of modern science and technology. When people are convinced that life can be changed, they are far more likely to experiment, take risks, and attempt to alter the course of things.

Since this view has predominated in Western culture for centuries, it is important that we take a close look at it.

An Evolutionary View of History

This linear view has been expressed in a number of different ways. One of the oldest and most enduring is the *evolutionary* view. Most of us already know something about the theory of biological evolution, but are surprised to learn that evolutionary ideas were applied to the study of history decades before Charles Darwin published his *The Origin of Species* in 1859. Georg Hegel, a German philosopher and university professor at the turn of the 19th century, developed a system of historical interpretation which did to historical events what Darwin later tried to do to biological forms.

Hegel believed that history is evolving through a series of conflicts which he called the "dialectic." According to his outlook, when an idea or movement (which he called the *thesis*) comes in conflict with its opposite (the *antithesis*), the resulting confrontation brings about something new which incorporates both the thesis and the antithesis, but goes beyond them (the *synthesis*). In time, this new idea or movement will come up against its opposite and a new synthesis will emerge.

Hegel's View of History

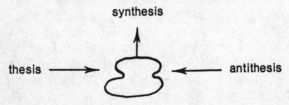

Through this constant dialectic, history proceeds. Hegel did not believe that this historical development was merely by chance, however. He argued that it was under the control of an Absolute Mind or Spirit which guided the dialectic toward perfection.

The Marxist View of History

Ordinarily, most evangelicals would pay little attention to Hegel's view, except that it has such a powerful heir: Marxism, an outlook which is making inroads in the underdeveloped parts of the world.

Hegel was willing to admit that the Absolute Spirit in control of the dialectic could be the Christian God, but there was nothing in his system which required it. Karl Marx, on the other hand, believed that economics, not the Absolute Spirit, was in control. More specifically, Marx argued that history was pushed along through a series of intense class struggles over the control of society's production and labor.

For Marxists, history is one long battle between the "haves" and the "have nots." During each successive historical age, the "haves" develop a social, political, and economic system for their own advantage. Eventually, however, their selfishness and corruption compel the "have nots" into open revolt. When the "have nots" overcome the "haves," they form their own society—and become "haves" themselves! Then the process begins all over again.

Using this basic dialectic approach, Marx believed that he could trace the course of human history. The earliest society, he said, was based on a primitive form of communism. Corrupt people, however, devised the concept of private property and destroyed communism, forming in its place a society based on greed and slavery. The slave society lasted until the Middle Ages when its "slaves" finally overthrew it and developed a different kind of economic order—feudalism. Feudalism endured for a few centuries and was replaced by capitalism.

As a member of a capitalist society, Marx (who lived in Europe during the middle of the 19th century) firmly believed that capitalism was already sowing the seeds of its own destruction. Very shortly, he predicted, the oppressed working class would rise in revolt and take control away from their capitalist overlords. Workers would then establish the "dictatorship of the proletariat," a transitional period of socialism during which the last stubborn vestiges of capitalism would be eliminated. Once that took place, Marx promised, a perfect, classless society would emerge in which all people would hold all things in common. In the new society each person would contribute to the good of the whole according to his ability, and receive from the whole according to his need.

Marxists believe that these "laws" of history are as firmly fixed as the law of gravity. We have all seen in our lifetime how this vision of the perfect future can motivate its adherents to dedicated and even fanatical action. Through legislation, subversion, and violent revolution, Marxists seek to cooperate with the historical process which is at work in the world. Convinced that they know where history is going, they carefully plan their present activities to help it along. No sacrifice is too great, no setback too disappointing to keep them from trying again and again to bring their program success. They believe they cannot lose because time and history are on their side.

A Christian View of History

Hegelianism and Marxism are not the only linear views of history available to people today. In fact, both are secularized versions of a much older view which predominated in Western civilization for a millennium before they were first articulated —the Christian view of history.

Most Christians think of the Christian faith primarily in individual terms, without realizing that it is concerned about far more than personal salvation. The Christian Gospel is also concerned with history. In fact, eschatology, the study of the end times, implies that there is also a beginning and middle to the story as well. Biblical eschatology is only the last chapter to the story of God's active and loving intervention in the universe which He created. Our Lord is not just concerned about His church, but the entire world. And the story which the Bible records is large enough to include all things. According to the Apostle Paul, the entire creation has been subjected to futility because of sin and will one day share in the grand finale of God's redemptive work (Rom. 8:18-25). In his letter to the Colossian Christians, Paul stated that the end result of Christ's work will be "to reconcile to Himself all things, whether things on earth or things in heaven, by making peace through His blood, shed on the cross" (1:20). God has an infinitely broad perspective. Not only is He concerned about saving individuals; He also cares deeply about history and the entire human story.

The Bible—A Story about God's Actions in the World

What would a person discover who picks up the Bible and reads it for the first time—without any preconceived notions about what he will find there?

Most likely he would conclude that he was reading a story about what God has done, is doing, and intends to do in the world. Furthermore, he would conclude that the story is told in a variety of ways. Sometimes it comes through books of history, but at other times, through beautiful poetry, wisdom literature, law, unusual biographies called Gospels, personal letters, and prophecies. Despite these different means of communication, the reader would have no trouble keeping the main story lines straight.

A loving and gracious God created the world out of nothing and made man (which He created male and female) in His own image, giving them dominion over all that He had made. Through a foolish and willful act of disobedience, the first man and woman sinned against God and thereby broke the fellowship which they had shared with Him, subjecting themselves and their descendants to alienation from God and spiritual death.

For man, this tragic state of affairs was irremediable. As fallen creatures, men and women could do nothing to bridge that gap between themselves and God which sin had created. But what man could not accomplish, God did. He devised a plan so extraordinary that, as the late C. S. Lewis has said, only God Himself could have come up with it. He would come to earth Himself, in the person of His own Son, to suffer the punishment and pay the price that His own righteousness required. All He would ask of people in return would be their acceptance by faith of what He had done for them. If people needed a bridge to span the sin chasm, then God would build it Himself.

The rest of the Bible records how God carried out His plan of redemption. He selected a man named Abraham and instructed him to leave his home and travel to an unknown land. He would become the father of a great nation through which the rest of the world would be blessed and saved.

God led Abraham to Palestine and established him there. His descendants, however, shortly moved to Egypt (for a number of reasons) where they prospered and multiplied. Observing their growing strength, nervous Pharaohs enslaved them and held them in bondage for centuries, until God raised up Moses, a Hebrew who had been a prince of Egypt, to lead the people out of slavery.

Following the exodus from Egypt, the children of Israel spent 40 years wandering in the wilderness while God instructed them in their special status as His people and revealed to them His Law. After a number of dramatic military victories, the nation took control of the land of promise which had belonged to Abraham. For a while, the people divided themselves into their respective tribes and were ruled by judges and prophets, but eventually three powerful and gifted kings, Saul, David, and Solomon, unified the twelve tribes of Israel and developed a rich and powerful nation. Their descendants, however, were idolatrous and corrupt. Political rivalries finally led to civil war and the division of the nation into northern and southern kingdoms.

What followed is one of the low points of the story. Despite the warnings of prophets sent from God, the people refused to repent and follow the faith of their forebears. After numerous attempts to bring Israel and Judah to their senses, God acted. The Assyrians and then the Babylonians invaded the land, devastated it, and carried the people into exile.

Even during the seven decades of captivity, the people remembered God's promises and longed to return to the Promised Land. But even after their return, God seemed silent and inactive. The land fell under the control of the Greeks, Seleucids, and eventually the Romans. Where was God? Where was His promised Messiah, the deliverer who would save the people and restore the kingdom?

When the time was right, God sent the Messiah—His Son, Jesus Christ. Born of a virgin, performer of miracles, authoritative teacher, He was the culmination, the focal point of God's plan of redemption. But He was not quite what the people expected. He came to suffer and die, not set up another political state. After running afoul of the Jewish leaders and Roman authorities, Jesus was put to death. Though the disciples at first believed the crucifixion was a terrible tragedy, because of Jesus' resurrection from the dead, they came to recognize it for what it was—God's way of paying the price for man's sin so that all people can be restored to fellowship with Him.

Here the story takes a completely unexpected turn. Instead of immediately setting up an earthly messianic kingdom, the resurrected and glorified Jesus told His disciples to wait for the Holy Spirit and then take the Gospel to the whole world. Thus empowered by the Spirit, the early church spread the message of Christ everywhere. Though God had originally chosen one group of people (the Jews) through whom to reveal Himself and His salvation, He was now making the Gospel available to all people through faith in Jesus Christ.

In the historical process, that is where the story now stands. God is building His church in the world. The Gospel is being spread to all people. But the story is far from over. The final chapter is revealed in the Bible's prophetic sections. In His grace, God has revealed how He intends to bring His redemptive plan to its fitting and final conclusion.

We have approached the study of biblical eschatology in this manner for a very practical and important reason: to show that biblical teachings on the last things must be seen in the context of God's entire redemptive work. Eschatology makes no sense at all unless we see it in light of what God has already done and is currently doing in the world. Even though eschatology is the final chapter of the story of God's ways in the world, it is only one part of the story. It is the capstone of God's plan of the ages which He devised and put into operation before the world began.

We have also attempted to demonstrate that our view of history—specifically how history is going to end—will determine in many ways how we live in the present. What we think will happen in the future should play a major role in how we organize and live out our days now.

The main theme of the final chapter in God's story is the second coming of Jesus Christ, and it's to that exciting event that we now turn our attention.

3

The Second Coming of Christ

The Second Coming of Christ is no secret to regular readers of the Bible. Jesus Himself spoke of His return and the events surrounding it many times during His earthly ministry, and the apostles made the Second Coming a major theme in their preaching and writing. The Apostle Paul, for example, referred to our Lord's return as "that blessed hope, and the glorious appearing of the great God and our Saviour, Jesus Christ" (Titus 2:13, KJV).

Despite its prominence in Scripture, the idea of the Second Coming is ignored, explained away, or denied by most people today. Why is this so?

Why People Deny the Second Coming

In his book *The Jesus Hope* (Downer's Grove, Illinois: Inter-Varsity Press, 1976), Dr. Stephen Travis of Great Britain suggests a number of reasons why the return of Jesus Christ is denied by so many people today. First, there is the problem of the Lord's long delay. As some people point out, the church has been waiting for the Second Coming for nearly two thousand years. Many, if not most, generations along the way have been convinced that they were the last before the Lord's return. How much longer, some people ask, will Christians continue to deceive themselves? If Jesus has not returned by now, chances are that He will not be coming back here at all.

There is certainly nothing new about this problem! The Apostle Peter reported that "scoffers" were already at work in his day asking, "Where is this 'coming' He promised? Ever since our fathers died, everything goes on as it has since the beginning of creation" (2 Peter 3:4). Peter's response to them is still valid for today: "But do not forget this one thing, dear friends: with the Lord a day is like a thousand years, and a thousand years are like a day. The Lord is not slow in keeping His promise, as some understand slowness. He is patient with you, not wanting anyone to perish, but everyone to come to repentance" (2 Peter 3:8–9).

Second, many people deny the doctrine of the Lord's second coming because it has so often been associated with fanaticism and bizarre behavior. In the middle of the second century, for example, three people from Asia Minor, Montanus and his two women associates, Priscilla and Maximilla, allegedly received divine revelations. According to these visions, Jesus' personal return was imminent and the New Jerusalem would shortly descend on two nearby villages. Despite official church condemnation, Montanus spread his message and built up a sizeable following. Eventually, the Montanist movement was fully discredited, but not before it brought about one of the first splits in the early church.

In the Middle Ages, there were a number of outbreaks of Second Coming fanaticism. According to a popular method of biblical interpretation, many people expected Jesus to return at the beginning of the earth's sixth millennium of history. (Didn't God create the world in six days and wasn't a day equal to a thousand years?) Since the creation of the world was set at about 4000 B.C., large numbers of people thought Jesus would return about A.D. 1000. As the year approached, thousands of people speculated about the identity of the Antichrist or made the long and dangerous journey to Jerusalem to be there when Jesus set foot on the Mount of Olives. Even when the year 1000 passed uneventfully, new dates were set throughout the 11th century.

In the 19th century, a strange case occurred when a Roman Catholic priest figured that Jesus would return in 1847. But by the time he secured his church's permission to publish his findings, it was already 1848.

Equally unfortunate were the efforts of Michael Baxter, a never-say-die Englishman, who made numerous predictions about the Second Coming between 1861 and 1908. At one point he argued that Jesus would appear on March 12, 1903 between 2:30 and 3:00 in the afternoon! Apparently only his death kept him from accumulating an even longer list of embarrassing failures.

By far the most publicized example of Second Coming mania occurred in the United States in the 1840s. William Miller, a Baptist preacher from Vermont, used his "millennial arithmetic" to determine that Jesus Christ would return in 1843. By the early 1840s, his movement had well over a million adherents in the northeastern United States. Even when the passing of 1843 forced Miller to set a new date (October 22, 1844), the enthusiasm only increased. As the day approached, millions of people made the necessary preparations. Though the stories of "Millerites" gathering on hills and rooftops in white "ascension robes" to meet Christ are not true, many Millerites did sell their farms, give away all their possessions, close their businesses, and let their fields go unharvested. Not surprisingly, when Jesus did not appear on October 22, the Millerites became a laughingstock. Excluded from churches because of their sincere but misguided fanaticism, the Millerites went their own way and founded the Seventh-Day Adventist Church, while other kinds of premillennialists struggled to regain a respectful hearing for their views within evangelical churches.

As painful as it is to admit, believers in the Second Coming frequently have been the doctrine's worst enemies.

Third, many people deny the possibility of the Lord's coming because it seems incompatible with a modern, scientific world view. Countless men and women equate belief in the Second Coming with an outmoded belief in ghosties and ghoulies, and things that go bump in the night. Modern folk, they argue, can no longer accept stories about miracles, demons, angels, and gods who return on the clouds of heaven.

From this perspective, it must be admitted, the Second Coming of Christ is not the primary issue at all—the whole supernaturalistic outlook of the Bible and the Christian faith is. Someone who rules out even the possibility of miracles or divine intervention in the world obviously cannot accept the idea of the Lord's return, just as he cannot consider seriously the concept of the Incarnation, the Resurrection, and the uniqueness of Jesus.

To these suggestions of Dr. Travis, we can add two more. Some people reject the notion of the Second Coming because it seems to be a novelty. In most Protestant and Catholic churches today, the doctrine of our Lord's return is never mentioned. A prominent authority in the study of American religion has said that he did not even hear about the premillennial return of Christ until he started graduate school—and he was reared in a mainline American Protestant denomination!

Finally, some people deny the Lord's return because they claim the term does not appear in the Bible. And they are right! "Second Coming" or "Second Advent" does not appear as such in Scripture, although the idea certainly does. The author of Hebrews, for example, states that Jesus "will appear a second time" (Heb. 9:28); and at the Ascension, the angels in attendance declared to the disciples that "This same Jesus . . . will come back in the same way you have seen Him go into heaven" (Acts 1:11). The teaching is there, even if the precise terminology is not.

Biblical Terminology for the Second Coming

If the authors of Scripture don't use such terms, which ones do they use to refer to the second coming of Christ? Four Greek words are consistently employed in this regard. *Parousia*, which means "presence, coming," or even "arrival," appears in such crucial passages as Matthew 24:27, 37–39; 1 Corinthians 15:23; 1 Thessalonians 2:19; 3:13; 4:15; and 5:23; 2 Thessalonians 2:1, 8; and 2 Peter 3:4. *Epiphaneia* means "manifestation" and is used in 1 Timothy 6:14; 2 Timothy 4:1, 8; 2 Thessalonians 2:8; and Titus 2:13. *Apocalypsis* is usually translated "revelation," but literally means a drawing away or laying bare—thus an uncovering of something which has been hidden from view. We derive our word "apocalypse" from it. This word is used to refer to the Second Coming in 1 Corinthians 1:7; 2 Thessalonians 1:7; and 1 Peter 1:7 and 4:13. The final word used by New Testament writers to refer to the Second Coming is the common verb *erkomai,* "to come." This word in its various forms is used about 700 times in the New Testament. On a number of occasions it is used for the Second Coming: John 14:1–3; Matthew 24:29–30, 39, 42–44; Mark 13:26; and Luke 9:26. A careful study of these words and their contexts reveals the following characteristics about our Lord's return.

1. *Personal.* Jesus *Himself* will return. The Second Coming does not mean Christ's coming for our souls at death, the outpouring of the Holy Spirit on the day of Pentecost, or Christ's involvement in historical events, such as the fall of Jerusalem. These are "comings" in a sense, but are not what the New Testament means when it refers to the Lord's return. In Scripture, the Second Coming points to Christ's coming at the end of the age—in person. As we already indicated, when Jesus ascended to the Father after His resurrection, angels told His disciples that the same Jesus who was now disappearing from sight into the clouds would someday return in the same manner (Acts 1:11). Furthermore, in writing about the rapture of the church, Paul stated that "the Lord Himself will come down from heaven, with a loud command, with the voice of the archangel and with the trumpet call of God" (1 Thes. 4:16). In the Olivet Discourse, Jesus said that after the Tribulation "they will see the Son of Man coming on the clouds of the sky" (Matt. 24:30). There can be no question: Jesus will *personally* return.

2. *Public.* The Second Coming will be no secret, "For as the lightning comes from the east and flashes to the west, so will be the coming of the Son of Man" (Matt. 24:27). As anyone who has lived on the Great Plains knows, it is impossible to hide a lightning storm! The Bible often uses dramatic picture-language to describe the extraordinary events of the end. When Jesus predicted the public nature of His return, He used a vivid passage from Isaiah 13:10: " 'The sun will be darkened, and the moon will not give its light; the stars will fall from the sky, and the heavenly bodies will be shaken' " (Mark 13:24–25). Many Christians want to know how literally to take such language. Is Jesus describing actual events which will occur at His coming, or is He using picture-language because no words are able to express the celestial signs which will accompany His return? Most Bible scholars believe the latter. No matter how we interpret passages of this nature, however, the main point is undeniable: Jesus' coming will be accompanied by unmistakable signs in the universe; no one will be able to miss His coming, even those people who are not expecting it. As Jesus said, the nations will be able to *see* the Son of Man coming on the clouds of heaven (Matt. 24:30). There will be no doubt that the Son of God has arrived.

3. *Powerful.* At His first coming, the Lord Jesus humbled Himself, took on the form of a servant, and even allowed evil men to put Him to death. Jesus' first advent was characterized by humiliation, lowliness, and rejection. The Son of God willingly laid aside some of His divine prerogatives (Phil. 2) when He took on the limitations of humanity. His Second Coming, however, will be far different. He will come in power, glory, and majesty, as befits the triumphant and resurrected God-Man. In the Olivet Discourse (Matt. 24; Mark 13, and Luke 21), Jesus plainly taught that His return will be glorious. Nowhere in the Bible is the majesty and power of the Second Coming more graphically described than in the Book of Revelation. As difficult as the Book is to interpret at times, one cannot possibly miss its overriding purpose—to show that the

lowly Lamb that was slain (Rev. 5) will become the conquering rider on the white horse whose name is King of kings and Lord of lords (Rev. 19). At the Second Coming, the world will not be able to reject or so easily dispose of Jesus as it did at His first coming. The time is approaching when "at the name of Jesus every knee should bow, in heaven and on earth and under the earth, and every tongue confess that Jesus Christ is Lord, to the glory of God the Father" (Phil. 2:10–11).

4. *Unexpected.* One of the most amazing things about the persistent attempts to set a date for the Second Coming is that Jesus Himself admitted that He did not know when it would be! "No one knows about that day or hour, not even the angels in heaven, nor the Son, but only the Father" (Mark 13:32).

Christ will come when people least expect Him. Jesus warned that "as it was in the days of Noah, so it will be at the coming of the Son of Man. For in the days before the flood, people were eating and drinking, marrying and giving in marriage, up to the day Noah entered the ark; and they knew nothing about what would happen until the flood came and took them all away. That is how it will be at the coming of the Son of Man. Two men will be in the field; one will be taken and the other left. Two women will be grinding with a hand mill; one will be taken and the other left" (Matt. 24:37–41). In a sense, it will be business as usual before Jesus comes. People will be going about their normal activities.

Most people today are totally oblivious to the fact of the Lord's return. If you are daring enough, try this little experiment: stop people on the street, in your neighborhood, or in the grocery store and ask them, "Do you think Jesus Christ will return to earth today?" Chances are that you will get some surprised looks and resounding "Nos!" That is exactly what Jesus meant. "The Son of Man will come at an hour when you do not expect Him" (Matt. 24:44).

Is it possible that some Christians might be surprised by Jesus' return? Probably. Many Christians conduct their lives as though Jesus were not coming back at all. That is why Jesus told His followers to keep watch, so that they, of all people, would not be taken by surprise. He instructed them about the end so that they would be prepared, no matter when it comes. Jesus illustrated the point by referring to the owner of a house who certainly would not have left his possessions unguarded had he known when the thief would arrive. "So you also must be ready" (Matt. 24:43–44).

Expectancy, watchfulness, readiness—these are the attitudes that Christians should demonstrate in anticipation of their Lord's return.

5. *Related to definite events.* The second coming of Jesus Christ will not take place in a historical vacuum. It will be closely associated with a whole series of predicted events.

Its relation to other events, however, does not contradict what we just said about its unexpectedness. Scripture does not give us the kind of information needed to calculate the time of the Second Coming, but it does give us enough information so that it will not take us completely by surprise. After discussing some of the events associated with our Lord's return (1 Thes. 4), the Apostle Paul reminded the church that "the day of the Lord will come like a thief in the night," but quickly added that "you, brothers, are not in darkness so that this day should surprise you like a thief. You are sons of the light and sons of the day" (1 Thes. 5:2, 4–5).

Specifically, the Second Coming will be preceded by the rise of Antichrist, the Tribulation, the rapture and resurrection of the saints, and will be followed by the Battle of Armageddon, the millennial kingdom, and the judgment.

Let's now examine some of the signs of the times to see how close we may be to the fulfillment of biblical prophecy.

4

The Signs
of the Times

"Christ's second coming is imminent. The signs are everywhere. Read the daily newspaper and see for yourself. Biblical prophecies are being fulfilled every single day before our eyes. Jesus may arrive at any moment."

We frequently hear that kind of statement these days. Each year scores of books are published and probably thousands of sermons are preached in an attempt to relate current events to some biblical prophetic scheme. How should we interpret the continuing Middle East crisis in light of biblical prophecy? What does the inevitable energy crisis have to do with the coming Tribulation? Is the European Common Market really the restored Roman Empire of the last days? In other words, to what extent can we find prophetic fulfillments in the events of our own day? Are the "signs of the times" that obvious?

Let's agree on one thing right at the beginning. There is nothing perverse about these questions. Anyone who firmly believes in the personal return of Jesus Christ to earth is naturally concerned about when it might occur. Christians would not be living up to Jesus' command to be watchful if they did not ask themselves such questions.

But history has shown that when Christians become overly concerned about the timing of the Second Coming, they get themselves into trouble. Setting dates and miscalculating the arrival of Christ have been the besetting sins of premillennialism over the centuries. Not only do such attempts bring considerable embarrassment and shame on the people doing the predicting, but they also discredit the doctrine of the Second Coming in the eyes of the rest of the world. As we observed in the last chapter, one of the main reasons many modern people tend to reject the idea of Christ's return is that a few believers in the past have made misguided and reckless predictions about it.

In case you are starting to feel a bit guilty about wondering about possible dates for the *Parousia* of Christ, take heart. The disciples shared your curiosity. On one occasion, they asked Jesus some specific questions about the divine schedule for the end of the age.

The Olivet Discourse

The conversation between Jesus and the disciples about the end times is known as the Olivet Discourse (because it took place on the Mount of Olives) and is recorded in Matthew 24, Mark 13, and Luke 21. As Jesus and His followers were leaving Jerusalem, one of the disciples, obviously impressed with the glories of the Holy City, pointed to the Temple and exclaimed, "Look, Teacher! What massive stones! What magnificent buildings!" (Mark 13:1)

The Jews had good reason to be proud of their Temple. Part of its exterior was covered with gold, and some of its stones measured over 30 feet in length. The Temple represented to the Jews a permanent symbol of stability and God's perpetual presence with His people. No doubt, then, the disciples were shocked and bewildered when Jesus replied, "Do you see all these buildings? . . . Not one stone here will be left on another; every one will be thrown down" (Mark 13:2).

The Temple torn down? How utterly incredible! How could the Jewish Messiah predict the destruction of the symbolic center of the Jewish religion? The disciples understandably wanted Jesus to elaborate on this disturbing prophecy, so when they had reached the Mount of Olives, some of them took Jesus aside and asked Him, "Tell us, when will these things happen? And what will be the sign that they are all about to be fulfilled?" (Mark 13:4)

When Christians speak about the "signs of the times"—evidence that Jesus' return is quickly approaching—one of the first passages they turn to is the Olivet Discourse. But before we can begin to examine Jesus' words in detail, we must underscore something which is usually overlooked in interpretations of this passage: the Olivet Discourse is *primarily* (though not exclusively) about the fall of Jerusalem and the destruction of the Temple—which occurred in A.D. 70. That the disciples had these events mainly in mind can be seen in Luke's account, which is almost exactly the same as Mark's: "Teacher, when will these things happen? And what will be the sign that they are about to take place?" (Luke 21:7) In their question, "these things" must refer to Jesus' prediction about the buildings being torn down (Matt. 24:2; Mark 13:2; and Luke 21:6).

But while the discourse is mainly concerned with the destruction of Jerusalem, it also looks beyond it to the end of the age and the coming of Christ. In Matthew's account, the eschatological dimension is clearly present: "Tell us . . . when will this happen, and what will be the sign of Your coming and of the end of the age?" (Matt. 24:3) This variation, however, does not contradict what we find in Mark and Luke. Undoubtedly, the disciples assumed the two events would occur at the same time. How could something as horrible as the fall of Jerusalem and the destruction of the Temple not take place at the end of the age?

Consequently in interpreting the discourse, we must keep this dual emphasis in mind: the historical fall of Jerusalem and the eschatological Second Coming. All of this makes the Olivet Discourse terribly complicated to figure out. The widely different interpretations by biblical scholars and teachers are ample evidence of that. But we can make things a bit easier by keeping in mind two common (though sometimes confusing) characteristics of biblical prophecy: the *foreshortening* of prophetic times and the *foreshadowing* of eschatological events in the events of history.

Let me illustrate the foreshortening of prophetic time in this way. I am writing this book from Denver, Colorado, which is located at the foot of the eastern slopes of the Rocky Mountains. Suppose I called friends in Chicago to describe the beauties of Colorado. I would probably mention our majestic view of Pike's Peak, Mt. Evans, and Long's Peak: three 14,000 foot peaks which can be seen from many spots in the metropolitan area. But if my description stopped there and my friends had never been to Denver, they would have no idea of how many other peaks, canyons, and meadows lie between the mountains I did mention. They would have to come West and hike or drive through the the mountains to fully understand how much territory there really is.

Biblical prophecy is something like that. Jesus and the prophets occasionally referred to certain prophetic peaks without mentioning all of the historical territory between them. As a result, the long stretches of time which separate the highlights of prophecy are foreshortened in such a way that they may seem brief or even nonexistent. In the Olivet Discourse, the fall of Jerusalem and the return of Christ seem to be close together chronologically, but as we know, 1,900 years have already passed between them.

Jesus nevertheless pointed out to the disciples that these two widely spaced events are closely related in their significance. In prophecy, historical events are frequently seen as partial fulfillments of future eschatological events. They are portrayed as foreshadowings of the events at the end of the age. In this case, the fall of Jerusalem and its accompanying horrors serve as dramatic symbols of the great Tribulation just prior to our Lord's return.

We have made this little detour for a very important reason: to show that we can't legitimately interpret this passage as exclusively a prediction about the fall of Jerusalem in A.D. 70, or the second coming of Christ at the end of the age. The

Olivet Discourse is about both. The trick, then, is to figure out when Jesus is talking about one or the other and to determine which signs belong to which event.

The Signs

In the first section of the discourse (Matt. 24:4–14, Mark 15:5–13, and Luke 21:8–19), Jesus gave His disciples a stern warning. "Watch out that no one deceives you" (Matt. 24:4). The purpose of the signs which follow, therefore, is to provide the disciples with enough information to keep them from being taken in by the disturbing events to come. But these signs do much more than that. They remind us of the underlying purpose of all biblical prophecy—to help us interpret the present, not forecast the future. Jesus gave His disciples this kind of information not just to satisfy their curiosity about future events, but to deliver them from paralyzing fear, and to stimulate watchfulness.

When most Christians speak of the "signs of the times," they have this passage in mind. It is crucial, therefore, for us to see exactly what Jesus had to say.

1. *False Messiahs.* The first sign has to do with the coming of false christs. "For many will come in My name, claiming, 'I am the Christ,' and will deceive many" (Matt. 24:5). Christians must be on their guard so that they will not be numbered among the deceived.

2. *World Conflict.* There will be armed conflict between nations and other kinds of political upheaval. "You will hear of wars and rumors of wars . . . nation will rise against nation, and kingdom against kingdom" (Matt. 24:6–7).

3. *Natural Disasters.* "There will be famines and earthquakes in various places" (Matt. 24:7). People by the tens of thousands, we may assume, will be greatly affected by these natural calamities.

4. *Persecution for Believers.* "Then you will be handed over to be persecuted and put to death, and you will be hated by all nations because of Me" (Matt. 24:9). Jesus elaborated more on this particular sign than any of the others. Persecu-

tion will come from all quarters; religious leaders, the state, and even friends and family members will contribute to the pain and suffering of the saints. "You will be handed over to the local councils and flogged in the synagogues. On account of Me you will stand before governors and kings as witnesses to them. . . . Brother will betray brother to death, and a father his child. Children will rebel against their parents and have them put to death. All men will hate you because of Me, but he who stands firm to the end will be saved" (Mark 19:9, 12–13).

Despite these terrors, Christians should not fear. When the time comes, God will give His children the strength they need and even the words to say so that they can endure—even unto death (Mark 13:11; Luke 21:14–15).

5. *World Evangelization.* In the midst of this terrible suffering, the Gospel will be spread throughout the world. As every student of church history knows, the church has often been most aggressive in its evangelism during times of persecution. Significantly, Mark placed this sign in the middle of Jesus' prediction about persecution: "On account of Me you will stand before governors and kings as witnesses to them. And the Gospel must first be preached to all nations. Whenever you are arrested and brought to trial, do not worry beforehand about what to say" (Mark 13:9–11). Matthew, on the other hand, placed it after the sign of persecution, but still closely related to it: "But he who stands firm to the end will be saved. And this Gospel of the kingdom will be preached in the whole world as a testimony to all nations, and then the end will come" (Matt. 24:13–14).

How should we take these signs? And even more important, how did Jesus intend us to take them? In the context of the whole passage, it seems clear that Jesus did not want His disciples to think that the end was immediately at hand. As He was relaying the signs, Jesus cautioned His followers not to read too much into them: "See to it that you are not alarmed. Such things must happen, but the end is still to come. . . . All these are the beginning of birth pains" (Matt.

24:6, 8). In other words, the signs in the Olivet Discourse are not signs of the *end* at all. They point to the *beginning of the end*, but not the end itself. This is clearly seen in Jesus' use of the term "birth pains" (Matt. 24:8; Mark 13:8). The idea of birth pains was frequently used in the Old Testament to refer to periods of crisis (Isa. 26:17; 66:8; Jer. 22:23; Micah 4:9). And it was common for Jews in Jesus' day to speak of the "birth pains" which would bring in the messianic age. In essence, then, Jesus was saying that when these signs begin to occur, we can be certain that "labor" has begun but had better not conclude that "delivery" is imminent.

If we understand this distinction, we will not make so many silly mistakes about predicting the end. Too many believers today contend that Jesus' coming is at hand because they can point to wars and the threat of wars, earthquakes and famines, the persecution of Christians in different parts of the world, and so on. The truth is that *every* generation from the early church on could make the same claims! There have always been wars and calamities in the world. In fact, natural disasters in the past make some of ours look like minor inconveniences. An earthquake in China during the 16th century killed over 800,000 people. An epidemic of the plague took the lives of over 75 million people in 14th-century Europe, while a famine in 1878 caused the starvation deaths of nearly 10 million Chinese. Clearly then, no single generation has cornered the market on wars, famines, or earthquakes. They have always been with us, and according to the words of Jesus, will always be so until the end.

How then should we interpret these signs? They are characteristics of the last days, which in the New Testament refers to the entire period between the first and second comings of Jesus Christ. On the day of Pentecost, for example, Peter claimed that one of the end time prophecies of Joel had been fulfilled (Acts 2:16). The rest of the apostles shared Peter's conviction that they were already in the last days (2 Tim. 3:1; 1 John 2:18).

We should not be surprised to see these signs in our own

time. That's as it should be. Such things as false messiahs, political turmoil, natural disasters, the persecution of believers, and the spread of the Gospel around the world are part and parcel of the way things are until the end. They are signs that the end has begun, but not that it is necessarily at hand.

The Desolating Sacrilege

Much more important in determining the nearness of the end is the desolating sacrilege which Jesus refers to in the second part of the discourse (Matt. 24:14–28; Mark 13:14–23; Luke 21:20–24). "When you see 'the abomination that causes desolation' standing where it does not belong—let the reader understand—then let those who are in Judea flee to the mountains" (Mark 13:14).

What is this "abomination"? According to Daniel's prophecy, which is where the term originates (Dan. 9:27; 11:31; 12:11), it refers to a profanation of the temple. When is this defilement to occur? Luke's account indicates that Jesus had the fall of Jerusalem in mind. "When you see Jerusalem surrounded by armies, you will know that its desolation is near. Then let those who are in Judea flee to the mountains, let those in the city get out, and let those in the country not enter the city. . . . Jerusalem will be trampled on by the Gentiles until the times of the Gentiles are fulfilled" (Luke 21:20–21, 24).

That's exactly how the early church interpreted the prophecy. When the Roman legions approached the city in the late A.D. 60s, Jewish Christians took the hint and left the city in droves, settling well across the Jordan. When the Romans finally breached the walls in A.D. 70, they desecrated the temple by carrying in their banners and insignia (which was considered sacrilege by the Jews), tore the temple down, set fire to its remains, and carried its sacred treasures back to Rome. If that's not a desolating sacrilege, what is?

Despite the accuracy of our Lord's prediction, the fall of Jerusalem did not completely fulfill our Lord's prophecy. Jesus looked beyond the events of A.D. 70 to the end of the age. "For then there will be great distress, unequaled from the beginning of the world until now—and never be equaled again" (Matt. 24:21). The fall of Jerusalem was bad, but it wasn't *that* bad. Jesus used the destruction of the city to foreshadow a worse calamity at the end of the age, the Great Tribulation.

The Coming of the Son of Man

In the third section of the discourse (Matt. 24:29–31; Mark 13:24–27; Luke 21:25–28), Jesus shifted His total attention to the end of the age. After seeing the fall of Jerusalem in A.D. 70 as a foreshadowing of the Tribulation of the end, He riveted His hearers with a prediction of His second coming.

"But in those days, following that distress, 'the sun will be darkened, and the moon will not give its light; and the stars will fall from the sky, and the heavenly bodies will be shaken.' At that time men will see the Son of Man coming in clouds with great power and glory. And He will send His angels and gather His elect from the four winds, from the ends of the earth to the ends of the heavens" (Mark 13:24–27).

Here is the foreshadowing and foreshortening that we discussed earlier. His original hearers could have easily misunderstood Jesus' meaning. They might have assumed that the glorious return of the Son of Man would follow the destruction of the temple. But from our perspective, we can clearly see that Jesus saw the fall of the city as a foreshadowing of something at the end of the age and foreshortened the time between it and His second coming.

The Fig Tree Illustration

Up to this point, Jesus had not directly answered the disciples' question about the time of His prediction. Most scholars will freely admit that the last section of the Olivet Discourse (Matt. 24:32–51; Mark 13:28–37; Luke 21:29–36) is one of the most difficult in all of prophetic Scripture. Consequently, the interpretation here is only tentative. But it's the best we can come up with in light of what we have already discovered about the discourse.

Concerning the time of His coming, Jesus said, "Now learn this lesson from the fig tree: As soon as its twigs get tender and its leaves come out, you know that summer is near. Even so, when you see these things happening, you know that it is near, right at the door" (Mark 13:28–29). The key to understanding these verses lies in the meaning of the phrase, "these things." Ordinarily, one would take it to refer to that which immediately preceded it, in this case, to the signs accompanying Christ's glorious return (namely, to the signs in the sun, moon, and stars). If this interpretation is correct, Jesus is saying that when people see these celestial signs, they can rest assured that He is on the way.

Those verses aren't too difficult, but those which follow have caused Bible scholars all kinds of trouble: "I tell you the truth, this generation will certainly not pass away until all these things have happened. Heaven and earth will pass away, but My words will never pass away" (Mark 13:30–31). In these verses, the problem lies in the meaning of "this generation" and once again "these things." Normally, one would take "this generation" to refer to those living in Jesus' day and "these things" to refer to the same things as in the previous verse. But you can see the problem: if we go along with that interpretation, then Jesus was obviously mistaken. The coming of the Son of Man did not occur during the lifetime of those hearing the prophecy on the Mount of Olives.

There have been many attempts to deal with this problem. As we might expect, liberal scholars claim there is no problem at all: Jesus was mistaken. He thought the end would occur within a few years, but obviously blew it.

Conservative scholars, on the other hand, have offered a number of other interpretations. Many evangelicals argue that "this generation" should be translated "this race." Thus Jesus is saying that the nation Israel (or the human race, as some contend) will not pass away before His *Parousia*. The Greek allows some justification for this translation, but it doesn't seem to make much sense. Is it really necessary for Jesus to predict that someone will be alive at the time of His appearing?

Another more recent evangelical interpretation contends that "this generation" refers to the last generation before Christ's return, whenever it may be. More specifically, a leading prophetic spokesman has argued that "these things" in this passage actually refers to the restoration of Israel to its own land, a prediction which does not appear in the Olivet Discourse *per se*. His contention is, therefore, that within a generation of the founding of modern Israel, the Second Coming will occur. Since Israel was established in 1948 and a biblical generation is roughly 40 years (Ps. 95:10), we should expect the Second Coming by 1987 at the outside, according to this view.

It is interesting to note that this same interpreter has recently advised that a biblical generation may be as long as a whole century, which would mean that he won't be here to take the ribbing in case he is wrong! At any rate, such speculation seems to go directly against what Jesus said immediately following the passage under discussion: "No one knows about that day or hour, not even the angels in heaven, nor the Son, but only the Father" (Mark 13:32).

There is another interpretation, however, which seems more appealing. It takes "this generation" in the normal sense of Jesus' contemporaries, but it holds that "these things" refer to the disciples' original question and the main point of the discourse—the fall of Jerusalem. According to this view, Jesus predicted that people then alive would live to see the destruction of the Temple, when "not one stone here will be left on another" (Mark 13:2). As we have seen, this is exactly what happened. Almost exactly 40 years after Jesus' words on the Mount of Olives, the city was destroyed by Roman legions! Here then is the answer to the disciples' original inquiry. When will the Temple be destroyed? Within one generation.

If this alternative is the correct one, then Jesus concluded His discourse with two separate but related comments about two separate but related events.

The Point of the Discourse

Strangely enough, Jesus gave His disciples some pretty definite information about the timing of the fall of Jerusalem, but He left them pretty much in the dark about the timing of His coming at the end of the age. As we have already seen, He stated that the time of the *Parousia* was the Father's secret (Mark 13:32). But that does not mean that believers should forget about it and live as though it probably will not occur in their lifetime.

The point Jesus wanted to stress was that His disciples should be watchful at all times. "Be on guard! Be alert! You do not know when that time will come. It's like a man going away: He leaves his house in charge of his servants, each with his assigned task, and tells the one at the door to keep watch. So you also must keep watch because you do not know when the owner of the house will come back—whether in the evening, or at midnight, or when the rooster crows, or at dawn. If he comes suddenly, don't let him find you sleeping. What I say to you, I say to everyone: 'Watch!' " (Mark 13:33–37)

What then can we say about the signs of the times? There are certain characteristics of the last days which we see continuing in our own generation. The fall of Jerusalem, which Jesus saw as a foreshadowing of the events of the end, occurred just as He said. All signs in the discourse, however, were not given for us to be able to calculate the timing of events. Signs of the times should help us get a proper perspective on life in the present. We don't have enough information for setting dates, but we do have enough to be sure that everything will come to pass as He promised. Are we in the last days? Yes. Is the Second Coming at hand? Only God knows for sure.

5

Antichrist and the Great Tribulation

Few topics in biblical prophecy have raised more questions or excited more interest than the Antichrist and the Great Tribulation. Two world wars, the Nazi extermination of 6 million Jews, the Korean and Vietnam conflicts, and the many guerilla and revolutionary uprisings since World War II have brought home to millions of people the reality of war and its horrible consequences. Therefore, people are intrigued, if not terrified, to learn that according to biblical prophecy, the worst is yet to come.

Similarly, people are fascinated by the prediction of a coming Antichrist, the Satan-inspired world ruler who will try to eliminate God's people and wage war on Christ Himself. Many people have wondered about his identity, and now even Hollywood has gotten into the act. In the mid-1970s crowds packed movie houses to see *The Omen,* a film depicting the Antichrist growing up as the son of the American ambassador to Great Britain!

Despite the popularity of such themes, we Christians must be careful how we deal with them. Some of us engage in rather wild speculation about events in the Tribulation. Most popular books on eschatology include elaborate maps of battles, identify all of the combatants, and boldly predict about what happens when. Educated guesses aren't totally out of place, of course, but they can be misleading when the guessers base their views on difficult and obscure passages. Usually they can't even agree among themselves—even when all insist they are interpreting the Bible literally.

The purpose of this chapter is simple: to relate what the Bible says about the Tribulation and Antichrist without going off the deep end. We won't try to identify the third toe on the right foot of Daniel's vision or speculate about the Beast's 10 horns and seven heads. In fact, I'm not certain anyone should, given the nature of biblical prophecy.

Biblical Apocalyptic

As we all know, the Bible was written in different literary forms: law, history, poetry, personal letters, and prophecy. Some prophetic books contain passages which biblical scholars classify as *apocalyptic literature* because of their general similarity to a form of Jewish prophecy (apocalyptic) which flourished in the centuries around the time of Jesus. That period was one of the toughest in Jewish history. God seemed distant and silent. The voice of prophecy was dead. The land was conquered and occupied by a series of godless powers. The people suffered persecution after persecution.

The faithful longed for divine deliverance, so a group of writers returned to the vision of Israel's prophets and predicted the imminent coming of the messianic kingdom and the destruction of Israel's enemies. To authenticate their work, they often wrote in the name of some Old Testament figure such as Enoch, Moses, Solomon, or Daniel. Since it wasn't safe to brazenly speak of the annihilation of their enemies, they concealed their message in the form of strange visions, revelations, and dreams which they related by extraordinary symbols and bizarre imagery. Apocalyptic literature abounds with incredible beasts, blazing celestial displays, and terrifying earthly calamities.

Most of our information about the Antichrist and the Tribulation comes from the Books of Daniel and Revelation, which contain such apocalyptic elements as symbolism and imagery. This is where we have to be very careful. We're right to assume that apocalyptic literature communicates real information, but we're wrong if we try to interpret it too literally.

Apocalyptic literature is very much like poetry in that it presents its truth differently than straight prose or historical narrative. Since both apocalyptic literature and poetry make their points in figurative and imaginative ways, one simply can't press every detail. For example, we can learn a lot from the Book of Revelation's description of the Antichrist, but we're missing the mark if we think we have to insist that he will actually have "ten horns and seven heads, with ten crowns on his horns, and on each head a blasphemous name" (Rev. 13:1).

Consequently, we can't expect to decipher every detail in an apocalyptic text. If we realize that the author of Revelation used symbolic picture-language and often shifted from one vision or scene to another with apparently little concern for exact chronology, then we won't become too dogmatic about our interpretations and insist that ours is the only one possible.

Because of the nature of this kind of literature, there are bound to be disagreements about what it means—even when we stay humble and resist the temptation to get pushy with our perspective. Unfortunately, evangelicalism is notorious for some of its squabbles over apocalyptic prophecy. The tragic thing is that while evangelicals disagree about the details of interpretation, they often overlook the fact that they are in hearty agreement on what the texts are really driving at—that despite every attempt of the Devil and Antichrist to subjugate the world, persecute God's saints, and thwart God's purposes, the risen Lord will preserve His followers and eventually gain a total victory over the powers of darkness. That much is plain to everybody. Perhaps we shouldn't expect total agreement beyond that.

Taking this somewhat cautious approach in interpreting apocalyptic prophecy, let's see what we can discover about the events of the Great Tribulation and about Antichrist who will dominate them. In order to get a well-rounded picture, we have to look at four important passages.

Daniel's Prophecy

The Antichrist first appears in Daniel's prophecy (Dan. 7–11). In a vision Daniel saw four strange beasts which symbolized four successive world empires. In addition to its iron teeth and bronze claws, the fourth beast had 10 horns. From these grew an additional "little horn" (7:8) which subdued three of the others and "made war with the saints and prevailed against them" (7:20–21, KJV). Daniel described the little horn in more detail: "He shall speak great words against the Most High, and shall wear out the saints of the Most High, and think to change times and laws; and they shall be given into his hand until a time, and times, and the dividing of time. But the judgment shall sit, and they shall take away his dominion, to consume and to destroy it unto the end" (7:25–26, KJV).

Here are the characteristics of Antichrist which other biblical writers develop in more detail: he is a blasphemer against God, a persecutor of the saints, a ruler who tries to bend the law to his own advantage, and a leader whose days are numbered and who will be utterly overthrown.

The Olivet Discourse

As we saw in the last chapter, Jesus referred to another prophecy from Daniel (9:27; 11:31; 12:11) in His discourse on the Mount of Olives. He spoke of an "abomination that causes desolation" which will introduce "great distress, unequaled from the beginning of the world until now—and never to be equaled again" (Matt. 24:21). Though this prophecy was partially fulfilled in the defilement of the temple by the Romans in A.D. 70 (Luke 21:20), Jesus was obviously looking beyond the destruction of Jerusalem to something far worse: "If the Lord had not cut short those days, no one would survive. But for the sake of the elect, whom He has chosen, He has shortened them" (Mark 13:20). That description could apply only to the Tribulation at the end of the age.

The Second Letter to the Thessalonians

The Apostle Paul gave us much more information about the coming of Antichrist and his reign. In his first letter to the Thessalonians, the Apostle described the Lord's return to gather living and dead saints to Himself (1 Thes. 4:13–18). But instead of taking hope and assurance from Paul's message, many of the saints became bewildered and afraid, evidently believing that the end was imminent and that the day of the Lord had already begun (2 Thes. 2:1–2). Paul forcefully countered this misunderstanding by reminding them that certain things had to take place *before* the glorious return of Christ. "Don't let anyone deceive you in any way, for that day will not come until the rebellion occurs and the man of lawlessness is revealed, the man doomed to destruction" (2:3).

This passage tells us a lot about the Antichrist. His chief aim is to acquire as much secular and spiritual power as he can. He undercuts all religion by outlawing any worship which is not directed to him as God (2:4). And he is empowered by Satan to perform "all kinds of counterfeit miracles, signs, and wonders" to deceive those who are perishing (2:9–10). In short, his entire personality and mission are seen as a revolt against the laws of God and man.

The revelation of Antichrist will be accompanied by "the rebellion" (2:3). The Greek word here is *apostasia* (from which we get "apostasy") which can be translated "falling away" as well as "rebellion" or "revolt." Some commentators who prefer "falling away" say that Paul was pointing to an apostasy of the church when many so-called Christians will reject the Gospel and turn to Satan. Some people claim to see such a movement already at work in the church. But what we see occurring today is a far cry from what Paul had in mind. This end-time rebellion is more than bad theology; it is a deliberate and defiant rejection of the entire Christian faith, not just its compromise on certain points. Most likely, then, the apostasy in the day of Antichrist will be a more generalized and all-encompassing rejection of God and the Gospel.

In a way, though, the rebellion will not be a totally new phenomenon in human history. Since the fall, the world has been in a state of revolt against God. Paul claimed that the "secret power of lawlessness" was already evident in his day (2:7), and the Apostle John warned that Antichrist's spirit is discernable in those who deny that Jesus Christ came in the flesh (1 John 2:18-23).

What's keeping this spirit of lawlessness from breaking out at any time? Paul said that some kind of force or power was holding it in check for the time being (2:6). He didn't clearly identify it, but added that "the one who now holds it back will continue to do so till he is taken out of the way" (2:7). Thus, Paul referred to this restrainer in two ways—as a *what* and a *who,* a power and a person.

What could Paul mean? There have been a number of interpretations. Many evangelicals insist that Paul was referring to the Holy Spirit. Once He is taken from the world (at the pretribulation rapture of the church), the lawlessness will be free to assert itself. Most exponents of this view believe that Paul is referring to the Spirit's active influence, not His actual presence. As they point out, in the Book of Revelation the Spirit supports and aids the saints who suffer at the hands of Antichrist, during the Tribulation and after the rapture of the church.

Another recent interpretation argues that the restraining force is the world mission of the church and the restrainer is Paul himself (or some other missionary). Advocates of this view use Matthew 24:14 for support: "And this Gospel of the kingdom will be preached in the whole world as a testimony to all nations, and then the end will come." As soon as the church finishes evangelizing the world, then Antichrist will be free to show himself.

A much older and possible view holds that Paul intended the Roman Empire (the restraining force) and the Emperor (the restrainer). In Romans 13 Paul argued that God had instituted human governments to keep the peace and preserve order in the world. They must punish the wicked and protect the righteous. Even bad governments (like Rome) managed to hold back the forces of anarchy and lawlessness. If this interpretation is correct, then Paul foresaw a time when human government will no longer be able to maintain control. The spirit of lawlessness which has always been evident in the world will finally amass enough strength to overthrow the governmental powers ordained to hold it in check. In Paul's day there was only one such governmental power—the Roman Empire as embodied in the person of its emperor.

The Book of Revelation

The final biblical passage dealing with Antichrist—the Book of Revelation—has more about the future than any other book in the Bible. And no other book has as much apocalyptic literature. In discovering its truth, we must not destroy its spirit. The Book of Revelation aims to stir our imagination and strengthen our faith, not provide a foolproof timetable for the future. Even though Jesus uses symbolic language to convey his message, we dare not pass it off as fantasy or the ravings of a first-century mystic. Revelation is an inspired glimpse into the future which describes real events in an imaginative and daring way.

In a vision John sees God on His throne holding a scroll with seven seals which contain the world's destiny (chap. 5). As the Lord Jesus opens the first six seals, a series of calamities strikes the earth: conquest, slaughter, famine, disease, martyrdom, and various earthly and heavenly events (chap. 6). Some scholars claim these disasters occur during the Tribulation, but they are probably similar to the signs in the Olivet Discourse which mark the beginning of the end and not the end itself (Matt. 24:4–14). Most likely, the Tribulation begins with the breaking of the seventh seal because after the sixth, people on earth declare that the day of God's wrath is about to begin (Rev. 6:15–17).

Before the last seal is broken, an angel puts the mark of

God on the foreheads of His people as protection from the judgments to follow (7:1–8). When the scroll is finally opened, seven trumpets are blown, each marking a terrible judgment on the earth. The first four affect the earth's environment (vegetation, the sea, rivers, and light); but the next two affect those who do not have God's mark. At the blowing of trumpet five, demonic forces are released to torment mankind; and at the sixth, a huge army from the east attacks and kills a third of the human race (9:1–19).

As with the seals, there is a break between the sixth and seventh trumpets. Two things occur which are a bit difficult to understand. The first is the "measuring" of the temple, which probably indicates God's intention to preserve the Jews for salvation; and the second is the ministry of two witnesses who prophesy on God's behalf until they are killed by the "beast" (who has not been introduced into the story yet—remember what we said about apocalyptic literature not being too concerned with exact chronology). After three days, God raises the two witnesses from the dead (Rev. 11:1–13).

Following this interlude, the seventh trumpet blows, announcing the end: "The kingdom of the world has become the kingdom of our Lord and of His Christ" (11:15).

The next section in Revelation discloses the worst part of the Tribulation. After giving God's people some additional encouragement (12:1–17), John describes the two central figures of this period: Antichrist and his false prophet.

The Antichrist is awesome: he is empowered by Satan, blasphemes God, gains unprecedented political authority in the world, is worshiped by everyone except the saints of God, and appears to be invincible (13:1–10).

Antichrist is assisted by a false prophet who serves as a chief minister of religious affairs. While the Antichrist handles politics, the false prophet takes care of religion. This points up one of the strangest features of the Tribulation era—it is an intensely religious time. The false prophet has the power to perform miracles to win people over to Antichrist. But in case that approach fails, he can resort to economic coercion:

anyone who does not receive the mark of Antichrist (probably some means of official identification) cannot buy or sell (13:11–17).

In a veiled way John identifies the Antichrist: "If anyone has insight," he writes, "let him calculate the number of the beast, for it is a man's number. His number is 666" (13:18). Few verses have triggered more speculation! In Greek and Hebrew, letters are used instead of numbers, each letter having a different numerical value (for example: A=1, B=2, C=3, etc). By adding up the numerical value of the letters in Antichrist's name, one arrives at 666. Who could it be?

Many scholars point out that the sum of "Nero Caesar" (the first Roman emperor to persecute Christians) in Hebrew is 666; and this seems to square with a common belief in the early church that Antichrist would be someone with Nero's spirit, or even Nero himself raised from the dead by Satan. But as church history testifies, one can do almost anything with numbers. During World War II, for example, it was pointed C=102), the name Hitler adds up to 666. A few years ago, some people devised a new formula to prove that Henry Kissinger, former U.S. Secretary of State, is the Antichrist. With that kind of human creativity, numbers don't really mean a thing!

As soon as John describes the Antichrist and the false prophet he announces their doom. God's wrath is poured out with a vengeance on all those who received the beast's mark. Seven terrible plagues affect the earth and escape is impossible: terrible sores, polluted seas and rivers, scorching sun, darkness (14:1—16:21). In this way "Babylon," the symbol of opposition to God, is finally judged (18:1—19:10); but not before an arrogant and satanic Antichrist tries one last time to put a stop to Christ. He gathers the armies of the world to battle the Lord of lords. The one who is called Word of God, however, easily conquers them at the last great battle in the world's history—Armageddon (19:11–21).

Thus the Tribulation ends. Antichrist and the false prophet are captured and hurled into the lake of fire; their armies are destroyed by a word from Christ; the saints who have endured the worst suffering in history are rescued. Suffering and endurance are replaced with honor and glory: "Hallelujah! For our Lord God Almighty reigns. Let us rejoice and be glad and give Him glory! For the wedding of the Lamb has come, and His bride has made herself ready" (19:6–7).

What about the Details?

Beyond that we have no desire to go. Though some believers attempt to get quite specific about the meaning of the various plagues or build massive arguments from obscure and symbolic passages, we have not. Apocalyptic literature does not lend itself to that kind of detailed interpretation. It seeks instead to paint in vivid and overwhelming language the events of the future. Though we often disagree on particulars of prophecy, its message is abundantly clear. Mankind's sin and rebellion against God will one day be focused in a brief period of anguish and suffering at the end of the age. Human sinfulness will have its final flowering in the person of Antichrist, who will attempt to control the earth and destroy the people of God. Despite this brutal and intense effort, God's people on earth will endure. Throughout the suffering of this Great Tribulation, they will cling to the promise that Christ reigns —and will shortly reign upon the earth. Their tribulation, though intense, will be brief. God has shortened the days. Antichrist may kill a number of God's people but he cannot stop God's purposes. In the end, God's people are victorious. They cannot lose. They have God's promise.

6

The Hour
of His Coming

Prophecy stresses that in the end Christ will triumph over Antichrist and the Devil, and be the undisputed Lord of all. Now it is time to see where the church, the Body of Christ, fits into the scheme of things. In the last chapter we saw how Christ will defeat the Antichrist at the Battle of Armageddon and rescue His saints who were under terrible persecution. Now we must try to determine who these saints are and how they are rescued. In other words, now we turn our attention to the Rapture and the Resurrection.

The "Rapture question" is the most hotly debated issue among American premillennialists. With a fervor that shocks Christians from other parts of the world, American evangelicals have divided churches, split denominations, and even ended long-standing personal friendships over whether Christ will come for His church before or after the Tribulation. In some quarters, one's view of the timing of the Rapture ranks almost with the inspiration of the Bible, the Virgin Birth, and the deity of Christ as a nonnegotiable fundamental of the faith. Some church leaders even refuse to appear on the same speaker's platform with anyone who doesn't share their opinion on this matter. We're not making light of the issue. After all, it could be a matter of life and death for some people!

We are disturbed, however, by some of the reasons people on both sides of the controversy give for believing what they do.

Believing for the Wrong Reasons

Some Christians believe the right things for all the wrong reasons, while other Christians believe things for no good reason at all. Here are some of the worst reasons for believing Christian doctrine:

1. *"That's what Dr. Bibfelt teaches and I trust him."* How often have you heard something like that? Many Christians attach themselves to a particular teacher or pastor and believe everything he says. They would no more doubt one of his opinions than debate one of the angels before the throne of God. No matter how unusual or "way out" the view, these rather gullible believers are willing to go to the stake—on their teacher's authority alone! How can they justify this kind of uncritical acceptance of everything they are told? "Dr. Bibfelt is such a godly man. How could he possibly be wrong about this when he is so right about everything else?"

2. *"But I need to believe it."* Some doctrines provide more emotional security than others. We probably all know people (outside the church, I hope) who refuse to believe there is a hell because they personally don't want to go there! Many Christians refuse to consider certain doctrines because they would cause them discomfort if they were true. I was once in a Bible study group on the Rapture question. One woman in the group refused to hear any view but her own. Her reason? "But I don't want to go through the Tribulation!"

3. *"That's what I've always been taught."* We all use this one occasionally; but in many ways this is the worst reason of all. Basically, it is an appeal to blind tradition. Don't get me wrong. I wouldn't be worth my salt as a church historian if I didn't recognize the existence of an authentic tradition. After all, we do speak of the *historic* Christian faith; and when we talk about history, we're talking about tradition. But there is a big difference in holding firm to the historic doctrines of

the faith and refusing to question what we personally have come in contact with. Like it or not, the real Christian tradition is bigger than our single congregation or even our particular denomination. We always have to recognize that what we've been taught may not always be what the historic church has taught. That doesn't mean we're slaves to the past and must adhere to the majority view on all matters. (If we decided eschatology by counting noses, then we'd all be amillennialists!) But it does mean that we must not be so narrow as to rule everything out just because it wasn't taught or preached to us.

The History of the Doctrine

Let's review some things from the first chapter. If someone had to go through the Tribulation, there would have been little or no argument: yes, they would. But in the late 1820s, John Nelson Darby, one of the leaders of the Plymouth Brethren movement, argued that the church will be raptured *before* the Tribulation even gets under way. He taught that God had two completely separate redemptive programs in history: one for an earthly people (Israel) and one for a heavenly people (the church). Once one had that principle in hand, the Bible took on a completely different perspective. All prophecies of earthly events belonged to Israel and all prophecies of heavenly events belonged to the church. To "rightly divide the word of truth" meant to keep the two peoples of God and their prophecies straight. Therefore, Darby and his followers reasoned, the saints who suffer during the Tribulation must be Jews because the suffering will take place on the earth. Where is the church? It must be in heaven, raptured before the prophecies of the Tribulation start being fulfilled.

Darby, a trustworthy and honorable man, visited the United States after our Civil War and won over some leading evangelical pastors and teachers to his point of view. From there the pretribulation rapture doctrine spread to Bible con-

ferences and institutes and through such popular books as the
Scofield Reference Bible. By 1900 American premillennialists
were clearly divided over the timing of the Rapture; and by
World War I there seemed to be more pretribulationists than
posttribulationists (namely, those who believe that the Rapture
will occur after the Tribulation). This situation prevailed until
posttribulationism began gaining ground after World War II.

Even though church history seems to indicate that posttribulationism prevailed until the early nineteenth century, it
can't make the final judgment on which view is correct. Only
the Bible can do that. Church history helps clarify issues and
determine who has the older view, but Scripture is our final
authority in matters of faith and practice. Let's look then at
some of the most important passages discussing the Rapture.

First Thessalonians 4:13–18

We begin with the passage which everybody can agree on! It's
so important that we'll quote it all:

> Brothers, we do not want you to be ignorant about those
> who sleep, or to grieve like the rest of men, who have no
> hope. We believe that Jesus died and rose again and so we
> believe that God will bring with Jesus those who sleep in
> Him. According to the Lord's own word, we tell you that
> we who are still alive, who are left till the coming of the
> Lord, will certainly not precede those who have fallen
> asleep. For the Lord Himself will come down from heaven,
> with a loud command, with the voice of the archangel and
> with the trumpet call of God, and the dead in Christ shall
> rise first. After that, we who are still alive and are left
> will be caught up with them in the clouds to meet the Lord
> in the air. And so we will be with the Lord forever. There-
> fore encourage each other with these words.

This is the clearest passage in Scripture on what will occur
at the rapture of the church: the Lord Jesus will descend from
heaven amidst the shout of command, the voice of the archangel, and the trumpet of God. Dead Christians will then be
raised up, followed by the transformation of those believers

who are alive. Both groups will meet Christ in the clouds.

When Christ comes for His church, this is what will happen. Everyone is agreed on that much. Notice, however, that Paul does not mention the Tribulation in this passage, so we must look elsewhere for the answer to when the Rapture occurs in relation to it.

The Olivet Discourse

As we saw in chapter 4, though Jesus was speaking primarily about the fall of Jerusalem, He looked beyond it to the Tribulation at the end of the age. Can we find anything about the Rapture in the Olivet Discourse? Jesus described His coming in much the same way Paul referred to the Rapture. "Immediately after the distress [the Tribulation] of those days . . . they will see the Son of Man coming on the clouds of the sky, with power and great glory. And He will send His angels with a loud trumpet call, and they will gather His elect from the four winds, from one end of the heavens to the other" (Matt. 24:29–31).

Notice the similarities in the Matthew and First Thessalonians accounts: both refer to Christ's coming and mention clouds, the trumpet call, the presence of angels, and the gathering of the elect. Posttribulationists conclude that both passages are describing the same event—the rapture of the church which comes (according to Matt. 24:29) *after* the Tribulation.

Pretribulationists admit that Jesus did not mention a pretribulation rapture in the Olivet Discourse. According to them, there was no need to. Christ had been describing a tribulation *on the earth* and thus was not talking about the church (God's *heavenly* people) at all. The gathering of the elect mentioned in Matthew 24:31 refers to Jews who had been converted to Christ after the rapture of the church and during the Tribulation.

Posttribulationists argue that this is reading something into the text which isn't there. They claim that the other position ends up with *two raptures:* one for the church before the Tribulation (1 Thes. 4) and one for Jews after it (Matt. 24).

Pretribulationists would rather speak of a *two-stage Second Coming* in which Christ comes *for* the church before and *with* the church after the Tribulation (when He will also rapture those who have been converted since the rapture of the church).

Second Thessalonians 2:1–17

As we noted earlier, Paul wrote this passage because the Thessalonians had become confused about Christ's return. "Concerning the coming of our Lord Jesus Christ and our being gathered to Him, we ask you, brothers, not to become easily unsettled or alarmed by some prophecy, report, or letter supposed to have come from us, saying that the Day of the Lord has already come" (2:1–2). He assured them that nothing could happen "until the rebellion occurs and the man of lawlessness is revealed" (2:3).

At first glance one might think that this passage poses major problems for a pretribulation position. If certain things must occur before the Day of the Lord, then an imminent rapture of the church is ruled out. But pretribulationists claim that the passage actually upholds their view.

First of all, pretribulationists insist that this passage must be taken in conjunction with others which seem to indicate that the church will escape the terrors of the Tribulation. After Paul's discussion of the Rapture (1 Thes. 4:13–17), dispensationalists point out, he assured the church that "God did not appoint us to suffer wrath but to receive salvation through our Lord Jesus Christ" (1 Thes. 5:9). Therefore, one must keep this teaching in mind when interpreting 2 Thes. 2.

Pretribulationists frequently bolster their argument by making a distinction between the term "Day of the Lord"—which they say refers to the period of judgment and glory initiated by His triumphant return at the end of the Tribulation—and "Day of Christ" which refers to Christ's coming for the church before the Tribulation begins. Consequently, they point out, Paul is stating that Christ can't come in glory until the Tribulation runs its course.

Furthermore, some dispensationalists say that *apostasia* ("rebellion," 2:3) can also be translated "departure" and thus refers to the Church's departure from the earth at the Rapture. In this case, Paul argues that the Day of the Lord cannot occur until the church is raptured and the Antichrist is revealed.

Posttribulationists, on the other hand, claim that this passage establishes their position beyond reasonable doubt. In the first place, they reject the "departure" translation of *apostasia* as highly unlikely and not supported by any other reference in the New Testament. Then they point out that there is no essential distinction between the "Day of the Lord" and the "Day of Christ." That which was called the Day of the Lord in the Old Testament (Amos 5:18; Zeph. 1:14) is called by a variety of names in the New: "Day of the Lord" (1 Thes. 5:2), the "Day of the Lord Jesus" (1 Cor. 1:8), the "Day of Jesus Christ" (Phil. 1:6), the "Day of Christ" (Phil. 1:10), or simply "that Day" (2 Thes. 1:10). All these, they claim, are interchangeable.

Additionally, they point out that the verb "gather together" in Matthew 24:31 has the same Greek root as "our being gathered to Him" in 2 Thessalonians 2:1, thus proving that the gathering of the elect by the angels after the Tribulation is the same as the rapture of the church which Paul described in 1 Thessalonians 4 and clarified in 2 Thessalonians 2.

To tighten their argument, posttribulationists ask a number of questions: If the church is to be raptured *before* the revelation of Antichrist, why didn't Paul say that the church's presence at Thessalonica was proof positive that the Day of the Lord had not arrived? If Paul wanted to ease the anxiety of the church, why didn't he come right out and assure the Thessalonians that they would escape the Tribulation altogether? If the church will be in heaven during the Tribulation, why did Paul even bother to describe the events of the rebellion and the revelation of Antichrist? Wouldn't such information be beside the point if the church were to be raptured before they take place?

Posttribulationists conclude, therefore, that Paul wanted to prepare the church for what was ahead and reminded them that before Christ's coming certain unpleasant things had to occur. The Day of the Lord wouldn't sneak up on them; they knew it was coming and knew what to look for beforehand (1 Thes. 5:1–11). Though God will allow the lost to be deceived by Antichrist (2 Thes. 2:10–11), He has chosen the saints "to be saved through the sanctifying work of the Spirit and through belief in the truth. . . . So then, brothers, stand firm" (2:13–15).

In other words, devout evangelical Bible scholars do not agree on the meaning of this crucial text. Both sides approach the passage reverently and carefully; and both feel equally justified in their conclusions.

The Book of Revelation

As we saw in the last chapter, the Book of Revelation provides us with the most information about the future. Though it describes the glorious coming of Jesus Christ in much detail (chap. 19), it nowhere explicitly mentions the rapture of the church.

The main issue, therefore, centers on the identity of the saints who suffer through the Tribulation. Pretribulationists, using their interpretative rule of thumb, say that since the prophecy concerns earthly events, the church must be ruled out. The saints, therefore, must be the Jews who accept Jesus as Messiah during the Tribulation, thereby incurring Antichrist's wrath. To substantiate this position, they point out that the 144,000 who receive the mark of God as protection against the judgments which are about to be poured out on the world (chap. 7) are made up of 12,000 from each of the twelve tribes of Israel. The rapture of the church, though it is not explicitly mentioned, must occur before the Tribulation gets under way. Most pretribulationists argue that it should occur before chapter 4 or else claim that the "Come up here" in 4:1 refers to the Rapture. Naturally, they are willing to admit, this is only an assumption based on an argument from silence.

Posttribulationists can't avoid arguing from silence either, because if their counterparts can't find a clearly stated pretribulation rapture, they can't locate a posttribulation rapture themselves. Their main argument is that the assertion that earthly events in prophecy can only apply to Israel, forces one to read things into the text and deny its most obvious meaning. After the letters to the seven churches of Asia Minor (chaps. 2—3), isn't it only natural to assume that the "saints" in the rest of the book are all those who believe in Jesus Christ, namely, Christians, both Jews and Gentiles?

Concerning the 144,000, posttribulationists point out that the twelve tribes of Israel (chap. 7) do not match any list of the tribes in the Old Testament (Gen. 49; Ezek. 48). The list in Revelation omits any reference to the tribe of Dan and actually counts the tribe of Manasseh twice, since Joseph (which Revelation lists as one of the tribes) was the father of both Manasseh and Ephraim, who is also not found on the list. Why did John, who was a Jew, include such a strange list? Posttribulationists argue that he did not want anyone to think he meant literal Israel, but the true Israel, all those who have the faith of Abraham and accept Israel's Messiah, Jesus (as Paul argues in Rom. 4 and Gal. 3).

At any rate, one can't decisively settle the timing of the Rapture from the Revelation of John alone. He must consult some of these other passages. Who is correct? We have not even begun to examine all of the arguments on both sides. You will have to decide for yourself.

The Resurrection and Rapture of the Saints

We argue so much about *when* Christ will return that we often forget that we all agree on *what* will happen at the hour of His coming: the resurrection of the believing dead and the transformation of those believers who are alive (1 Thes. 4).

In the sequence of events, the resurrection comes first. At His *Parousia,* Christ will raise up the saints, which will include those from the Old Testament era. But what kinds of bodies will the dead receive?

Paul declares that they will be like Christ's resurrection body (Phil. 3:21). After He rose from the dead, our Lord's body was similar to, yet vastly different from, His former one. It was obviously a real body: His disciples recognized Him, touched Him, and ate with Him. But the Lord's resurrection body was also radically different: He could pass through solid doors and walls and come and go at will (John 20—21).

Our bodies will be like that. In his chapter on the Resurrection, Paul describes them as imperishable, glorious, powerful—"spiritual" (1 Cor. 15:42–44). They will be incapable of decay, sin, or failure. They will be like Christ's.

We must not underestimate the importance of this coming event. The biblical doctrine is resurrection of the body, not only immortality of the soul. God plans to provide us with bodies, not allow us eternally to float through the universe as disembodied spirits. In a real sense, our redemption will not be complete until we receive bodies like our Lord's.

That raises a question about the "intermediate state"—that period between death and the resurrection. What happens then? There is no evidence in the Bible for any kind of unconscious "soul sleep." The truth is that Scripture does not give us much information about this period. About all Paul says about it is that to be absent from our earthly bodies is to be present with the Lord (2 Cor. 5:1–9). It is useless to speculate about it. All we can do is be confident that at death we are in God's presence and that we will receive our new bodies at the coming of Jesus Christ.

But what if we are still alive at Christ's return? Obviously, only the dead can be resurrected. The rest of us will be transformed, given "resurrection" bodies without having to pass through death. (Strictly speaking, only this second event at Christ's *Parousia* is called the Rapture.)

Listen to Paul: "I tell you a mystery: We shall not all sleep, but we shall all be changed—in a flash, in the twinkling of an eye, at the last trumpet. For the trumpet will sound, the dead will be raised imperishable, and we shall be changed. For the perishable must clothe itself with the imperishable, and the mortal with immortality" (1 Cor. 15:51–53).

At the *Parousia,* the dead in Christ will be resurrected, but those who are alive in Christ will be transformed into the same kind of spiritual bodies without passing through death. The dead look forward to the resurrection and the living wait for their transformation at the Rapture.

What is in store for the saints after these glorious events? Revelation speaks of "two resurrections" with a long period of time in between. Let's examine the last chapter in God's redemptive plans—the Millennium and the Last Judgment.

7

The End of the Story

Despite the difficulty in interpreting certain prophetic texts, the Bible's main message is clear: Jesus Christ will personally and dramatically break into history to put a stop to Antichrist, the false prophet, and their supporters. But that is not the end of the story. Jesus is returning to more than destroy Antichrist's domain. He's coming back to establish one of His own. The story of God's plan for the end of the age would not be complete without a discussion of the Millennium (Christ's 1,000-year reign on earth) and the Last Judgment.

In the last chapter we looked at some of the various positions on the Rapture. Because disagreements about its timing are so intense, many evangelicals assume that the Rapture is the most controversial topic in biblical prophecy. But church history shows that first place in that category goes to the Millennium. In fact, historians of doctrine will classify the major systems of eschatological interpretation by what Christian teachers do with it.

The only passage in the Bible to mention the 1,000-year reign of Christ explicitly is Revelation 20:1–10, and there the Millennium (*mille* is Latin for "thousand") is seen primarily against the backdrop of Satan's destruction.

Before we examine the different interpretations of this crucial passage, we have to make sure we know what it's all about. In a nutshell, John envisioned that after dispensing with the beast, the false prophet, and their armies (19:11–21), the Lord would direct His attention to giving the devil what he deserves. Unlike the others, however, the devil's doom will come in two installments. First, at Christ's coming, an angel binds Satan and imprisons him in an abyss "to keep him from deceiving the nations any more until the thousand years were ended" (20:3). While the devil is thus detained, Christ and His saints reign; but after the Millennium, Satan is released to deceive the nations one last time. After he stirs up a short-lived rebellion against King Jesus, Satan is cast into the lake of fire where he joins his old allies, Antichrist and the false prophet, in order to "be tormented day and night forever and ever" (20:10).

No one doubts that this is what the text *says,* but Christians have never been able to agree on what it *means.* Because apocalyptic literature is hard to interpret in detail, it's not surprising that believers over the centuries have understood this passage differently. Traditionally, they have chosen one of three alternatives.

Postmillennialism

Naturally, how one approaches John's Revelation as a whole will determine to a large degree how one interprets its passage on the Millennium. One group of Christians sees Revelation as a prophecy which depicts in symbolic form the entire course of the Church Age, not just a relatively brief period at its close. To them, the Millennium represents a literal period of peace which will occur once the majority of mankind accepts Jesus Christ. As the church evangelizes the world and more people embrace the Gospel, then all of society will be progressively "Christianized." In this manner Satan is "bound" and his influence over the nations effectively eliminated.

After 1,000 years of this earthly kingdom of God, Satan will launch a rebellion to undo what the church through the Spirit's power has accomplished. This satanic revolt is the

Great Tribulation, which will be brought to an end by the personal return of Jesus Christ to raise the dead, judge the world, and usher in the new heavens and the new earth (the eternal state).

Because these Christians do not expect Christ's second coming until *after* the Millennium, they are called *postmillennialists.*

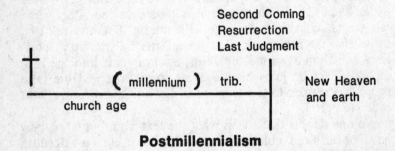

Postmillennialism

A type of postmillennialism was popular in the Middle Ages, but its greatest popularity occurred from the middle of the 1700s to the beginning of the 1900s—in the United States! Jonathan Edwards, the great Puritan preacher, theologian, and revivalist, proclaimed in his *History of the Work of Redemption* (1739) a postmillennial Second Coming. Recent revivals in New England had convinced him that the Millennium was near and that "there are many things that make it probable that this work will begin in America."

Edwards' postmillennial interpretation caught on in American evangelicalism and became the most prominent view during the 1800s. Charles Grandison Finney, for example, America's greatest revivalist in the first half of the 19th century, declared in 1835, "If the church will do her duty, the Millennium may come in this country in three years."

Christians with this kind of optimism naturally worked very hard to bring in the Millennium which seemed just around the corner. They held evangelistic campaigns, organized missionary societies, and founded social reform movements in an attempt to Christianize the world. The "social gospel" movement, which began to flourish at the end of the century, was in part an expression of postmillennialism.

One can easily imagine what World War I did to the popularity of postmillennialism in the churches. The horrors of world war, along with a number of other social, political, and economic crises in the early 20th century, convinced most people that things were getting worse, not better, and that the Millennium was nowhere in sight.

Amillennialism

Whereas the postmillennialists believe that there will be a literal Millennium on the earth, another group of Christians are convinced that there will never be such an era—before or after Christ's second coming. For that reason, their view is called *amillennialism,* which means "no-millennialism."

As with the first group, they arrive at their view of the Millennium through their basic approach to Revelation. Instead of seeing the book as a forecast of the historical events of the Church Age, amillennialists believe it is a symbolic representation of the Christian life and the spiritual battles between the children of God and the powers of darkness. They interpret the Millennium as the spiritual reign of Christ between His resurrection and His Second Coming.

During His earthly ministry, the amillennialists believe, Jesus bound Satan so that he could no longer deceive the nations. He still had the power to mislead individuals, but he lost the ability to keep whole nations in the dark. That Gentiles now receive the Gospel is proof of that. Anyone who accepts the reign of Jesus in his life is therefore in the Millennium. During the Church Age those who die in Christ reign with Him on His spiritual throne in heaven, but as soon as a person is converted (which amillennialists equate with the "first resurrection" in Revelation 20:5), he starts to experience the millennial reign of Christ in his own life.

At the end of the Church Age (amillennialists don't take the thousand years literally), Satan will be loosed to deceive the nations once again. The revelation of Antichrist will then ensue, along with the Great Tribulation. Both will come to an end at Christ's personal second coming, following which there will be the general resurrection of the dead, the last judgment, and the beginning of the eternal order—but no earthly kingdom.

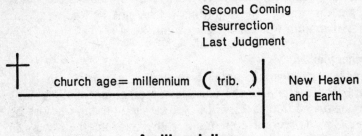

Amillennialism

This view seems to have originated with Augustine, the prominent theologian and bishop of the late fourth century. Since the Christian church had already reached official status in the Roman Empire, Augustine assumed that the days of persecution were over and equated the kingdom of God with the church. He spiritualized the Millennium as the heavenly reign of Christ and the departed saints during the Church Age. Augustine interpreted the thousand years literally and predicted the Second Coming around A.D. 1000, but when the year passed uneventfully, amillennialists decided that the number should be taken figuratively too.

Amillennialism predominated during the Middle Ages and was the majority view during the Protestant Reformation.

Such Protestant leaders as Martin Luther and John Calvin condemned the idea of a literal Millennium as a foolish throwback to Jewish hopes. The leading Reformation confessions of faith were amillennial, and most of them stated clearly their dislike for the doctrine of an earthly millennial reign of Christ. One Reformed Confession (the Helvetic Confession, article XVII) condemned "the Jewish dream of a Millennium, or a golden age on earth, before the last judgment."

Amillennialism remains the majority view among the world's Lutherans, Presbyterians, Reformed, and Methodists (not to mention the Roman Catholics). America's largest evangelical · denomination, the Southern Baptists, is overwhelmingly amillennial.

Premillennialism

In contrast to these two positions, a third group of believers interprets Revelation as a prophecy of the closing years of the Church Age whose events are yet to be fulfilled. These Christians take the Book more literally than the others and therefore view the Millennium as an actual earthly kingdom which will be established by the returning Son of God. Since this viewpoint expects Christ to come *before* the setting up of the kingdom, it is called *premillennialism*.

Premillennialists point out that the passage on the Millennium should not be isolated, but taken in the broader context of Christ's final victory. In other words, they believe that Revelation 19:11—20:10 should be taken as a single unit. The defeat of Antichrist and the false prophet (19:17–21) and the destruction of their mentor, Satan (20:1–10), should be seen as part of the same triumph of the returning King of kings and Lord of lords (19:11–16). Because Christ's victory over the beast, false prophet, and Satan are actual events in history, there is no reason to doubt that the reign of Christ and His saints will also be an actual historical event.

Consequently, premillennialists teach that at the Second Coming our Lord will defeat Antichrist and his supporters, bind Satan, and establish an earthly kingdom which will last for a millennium. At the conclusion of the 1,000 years, Satan will be allowed one last rebellion, then will be cast into the lake of fire. Christ will then resurrect the dead (Christians will already have been raptured and resurrected at the Second Coming before the Millennium) for the Last Judgment, which will be followed by the formation of the new heavens and the new earth.

Premillennialism

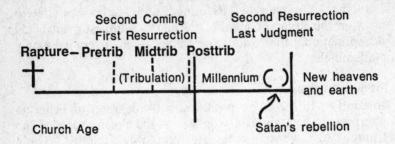

From every indication, premillennialism was the view of the early church, though we must admit that at times the kind of premillennialism held by some of the early church fathers appears quite different from more recent varieties. A number of factors contributed to its demise: extremism among some of the early premillennialists (the Montanists, whom we have already mentioned, and an overly "materialistic" emphasis); the close association between the church and the state which followed the Emperor Constantine's "conversion" to Christ in the early fourth century convinced many believers that they should not expect a tribulation in the future and they were already in the Millennium.

Premillennialism started making its comeback in the early 1800s when the French Revolution and other events quickened an interest in biblical prophecy. As we have already seen, premillennialism received its greatest boost when one of its more recent forms, dispensationalism, came to the United States after the Civil War and spread by means of Bible and prophetic conferences, popular teachers, and their books.

It would be safe to say that most people who trace their roots to the fundamentalist movement maintain premillennialism in one form or another.

A Closer Look
Let's explore Scripture in more detail to see what we can learn

about the coming Millennium and the events which follow.

1. *The Binding and Loosing of Satan.* The Millennium is bracketed by the imprisonment and release of Satan (Rev. 20:1–3, 7–10), and this raises all kinds of questions. Who are the nations which the devil is kept from deceiving? If Antichrist and his followers are destroyed at Christ's *Parousia,* then who will be left? If Christ has ruled in righteousness for a millennium, how will Satan be able to mount a revolt against Him?

Though Antichrist's domain will be extensive, evidently it will not embrace the entire world. There will be nations which will manage to remain outside the struggle between the Antichrist and the returning Lord. The nations which are not destroyed at Armageddon will thus need protection from the devil's deception, and it will be for their sakes that Satan will be bound.

The existence of these nations within Christ's millennial kingdom accounts for Satan's ability to stir up a revolt after his release. Though these people will be under Jesus' control, obviously some of them will not be committed to Him as Lord. The Devil will be able to arouse their unregenerate hearts to revolt against the King of kings.

2. *The Reign of Christ and His Saints.* Despite the mention of a 1,000 year reign, Revelation 20 provides little information about the Millennium: "I saw thrones on which were seated those who had been given authority to judge. And I saw the souls of those who had been beheaded because of their testimony for Jesus and because of the Word of God. They had not worshiped the beast or his image and had not received his mark on their foreheads or their hands. They came to life and reigned with Christ a thousand years" (Rev. 20:4).

This is a difficult verse and interpreters have disagreed on its meaning. Most likely this scene depicts two groups: the saints in general, and those who had been martyred during the Tribulation, who receive special recognition. Throughout the Old and New Testaments, the saints of God are promised a share in the reign of Christ. Daniel, the prophet, stated that at the coming of the Son of Man, the saints will be given a kingdom and all dominions shall serve and obey them (Dan. 7:27). Jesus promised that when He sat on His glorious throne, His followers would have thrones of their own besides (Matt. 19:28). And Paul simply asked the Corinthian church, "Do you not know that God's people will judge the world?" (1 Cor. 6:2). Thus Christ will share His millennial reign with His saints.

Many questions remain unanswered: What will be the relationship between the saints (who all have resurrection bodies) and the world's population? What will the reigning saints do for 10 centuries? What will the world be like under the personal rule of Jesus Christ? What is the place of the Jewish people in the Millennium?

Premillennialists have answered these questions in a variety of ways. For a description of world conditions in the Millennium, many premillennialists refer to certain Old Testament passages which predict (in quite figurative language) the glories of the coming messianic kingdom: universal peace (Isa. 2:4; Micah 4:3–5), a restoration and pacification of all nature (Isa. 11:6–9), a complete lack of false religion (Zech. 13:2), and even expanded life spans (Isa. 65:20). Naturally, it is hard to know how far to press these details. Nevertheless, the point is clear—under the reign of Jesus Christ, all aspects of life will be as they should. The world will experience, for the first time since the Fall, a social order in which God's will is done as it is in heaven. All of the dreams of mankind for social justice, racial equality, economic fairness, and peace will be realized. Instead of political leaders who deal falsely with their constituents and use power to their own advantage, the Lord Jesus Christ will be at the reins of government. Language is probably incapable of describing the resulting improvements in human life.

Premillennialists are divided over the Jews' role in the coming Millennium. One variety of premillennialism, dispensationalism, sees the 1,000-year reign in terms of a Jewish kingdom in which all of the theocratic promises to Israel are literally fulfilled. These believers expect a restored Davidic kingdom, the rebuilding of the Jerusalem temple, and the restoration of the sacrificial system. As we have seen, dispensationalists interpret Revelation as a prophecy of what will happen to a faithful remnant of Jewish believers after the rapture of the church.

Nondispensational premillennialists, on the other hand, view the Millennium in terms of the people of God as a whole and not just the Jewish people. They expect a massive turning to Christ among the Jews (probably during the Tribulation), but see Old Testament prophecies to Israel fulfilled finally for the New Israel, which is made up of Jews and Gentiles who have placed their faith in Jesus.

3. *The Two Resurrections.* Revelation 20 refers to two resurrections which occur before and after the Millennium (20:4–6). The first resurrection will consist of the saints at Christ's second coming (see 1 Thes. 4:13–17; 1 Cor. 15:50–57). The second resurrection will occur after the Millennium for all those who died without Christ. The purpose of the two resurrections seems clear: the first will occur so that those who have died in Christ can experience the final triumph of their Lord; the second will occur as a necessary prelude to judgment.

One can easily see the benefits to being part of the first resurrection. "Blessed and holy are those who have part in the first resurrection. The second death has no power over them, but they will be priests of God and of Christ and will reign with Him for a thousand years" (Rev. 20:6).

4. *The Last Judgment.* After the Millennium and the destruction of the devil, the Last Judgment will take place (Rev. 20:11–15). Few topics are avoided more than this one. Granted it is not a very pleasant subject, but it is an integral part of the biblical message.

Accountability is a built-in part of the moral order which God has created: "Do not be deceived: God cannot be mocked. A man reaps what he sows" (Gal. 6:7). Consequently, judgment is one appointment no one will be allowed to skip: "A man is destined to die once, and after that to face judgment" (Heb. 9:27).

In John's Revelation, judgment consists of the opening of books in which the deeds of individuals have been recorded. Nowhere in the text does it say that anyone will be saved by his works. This will come as a cruel blow to those who have been trying to earn their salvation by doing good deeds. As Paul stated, "Clearly no one is justified before God by the Law, because, 'The righteous will live by faith' " (Gal. 3:11).

There is another way. Those whose names are written in the Book of Life will be saved. Such a book is mentioned frequently in the Bible (Dan. 12:1; Luke 10:20; Phil. 4:3) and refers to all those who are saved by faith in the Messiah. Those whose names are not included in this Book are cast into the lake of fire, along with death and Hades.

There is nothing pleasant about this passage; and there is no use speculating about the geography of hell or the temperature of the flames. The picture the Bible paints is graphic enough. In the end, God will not only punish the devil and his chief henchmen, but He will similarly treat those who have aligned themselves with Satan in one way or another—which includes everyone who has not afforded himself of the Gospel through faith. Those individuals will suffer the "second death."

5. *The New Heaven and Earth.* The ultimate destiny of God's redeemed people will be a new heaven and earth. According to John's Revelation, the eternal state will not consist of our flying from cloud to cloud; it will take place on a newly created earth (Rev. 21:1—22:6). Here again the details are highly figurative, but the message is clear: God's ultimate purpose includes the total refashioning of the physical universe as an eternal dwelling place for His people.

This point needs some clarification. In the New Testament, the *heavenly* Jerusalem is only the temporary dwelling place for the Christian between his death and the resurrection (Heb. 12:22; Phil. 1:23; 3:20). But after the resurrection and the final judgment, the heavenly Jerusalem will descend in order to be permanently located on the new earth (Rev. 21:1–5).

The story is now complete. Christ has come, rescued and redeemed His people, defeated the powers of darkness, concluded His earthly reign, and conducted the final judgment. He has created a new heaven and earth for an eternal dwelling place.

The Bible's eschatological promise and perspective are immense. It's all a bit overwhelming when one tries to take it all in. What should we say in response? Perhaps nothing is a better response than one of the praises from Revelation: "Allelujah: for the Lord God omnipotent reigneth. Let us be glad and rejoice, and give honor to Him. . . . Amen. Even so, come, Lord Jesus" (Rev. 19:6–7; 22:20, KJV).

8

Thy Kingdom Come

Now that we have outlined the basic events surrounding the second coming of Christ, we must deal with an equally important issue—the practical consequences of biblical eschatology. When studying Scripture, Christians should always have two questions in mind: What does the Bible actually teach? And, what difference should this teaching make in daily living?

Many Christians seem content with just knowing what the Bible teaches without ever thinking about the practical implications of their beliefs. Though this is common, it is hardly the biblical pattern. According to Scripture, the Christian hope should have a direct bearing on the Christian life. The study of eschatology should lead to an improvement in a believer's behavior. It should not merely satisfy his curiosity about the future or rearm him against fellow believers who disagree with his interpretation of prophetic passages.

Scriptural teaching never lets us forget that eschatology is practical. The Apostle Peter, for example, after describing the terrible destruction to follow the Day of the Lord, asked: "Since all these things are to be destroyed in this way, what sort of people ought you to be . . .?" (2 Peter 3:11, NASB) Similarly, John put the Christian hope in personal and practical terms: "Everyone who has this hope fixed on Him purifies himself, just as He is pure" (1 John 3:3, NASB).

Believers who spend all their time on the *what, when,* and *how* of prophecy, and ignore the *so what,* are distorting the biblical balance. Our study of the future is never complete until we apply it to the present.

Seeing Ourselves as Others See Us

If doctrine and duty are dual emphases in Scripture, we must constantly check to see if our beliefs are properly affecting our behavior. One way to do this is to discover how we come across to people who do not necessarily share our convictions. Often we can learn more from our critics than from our friends. How do we appear to nonbelievers or other Christians who don't share our eschatological views?

Our opponents have criticized us in two ways. The first has to do with inconsistency: we premillennialists don't act as though we really believe Christ will return soon to set up His kingdom. We proclaim the message but live as though He were not coming back at all. A postmillennialist at the turn of the century claimed that the only thing distinctive about premillennialists' behavior was their constant attendance at prophetic conferences and their persistent attempts to prove that everybody else had misinterpreted the Bible!

The second charge centers on an alleged lack of concern for the present: premillennialists are so occupied with the future that they frequently fail to see and do anything about the urgent needs of the present.

At first glance these two charges seem contradictory: how can we be uninterested in the present and at the same time conduct our present lives like the rest of the world? Let's explore the charge that premillennialists pay little attention to the present age.

What Can You Expect?

Most of us would agree that people should be judged only when they fail to accomplish what they *ought* or *are able* to do. It is unfair to hold people responsible for not doing the impossible or failing to do things which are not required. Many premillennialists believe that God does not want or expect believers to become involved in this evil age. The kingdom of God, they say, is entirely future and totally dependent on the return of the Lord Jesus. Therefore, Christians must not act as though it were already here.

According to this point of view, the present age belongs to the devil. God has washed His hands of this dispensation, giving Satan full rein until the Second Coming. Under these conditions, attempts at long-range social reform are fruitless and even compassionate social concern runs the risk of deterring believers from their primary responsibility—evangelizing the lost before it is too late. Though they sincerely grieve over current problems, these premillennialists firmly believe that they can do nothing about them. In fact, some premillennialists who hold this point of view warn that anyone who tries to change the downward course of this age or alleviate the Satan-caused problems around him is actually playing into the devil's hands and thwarting God's purposes for this age.

These premillennialists believe that Christians who do not become actively embroiled in the present decline should not be condemned; they should be praised for fulfilling their proper, God-given roles. Christians are called to evangelize the lost and separate themselves from the world.

The Present and Future Kingdom

As popular as this perspective has been in Christian circles, it is a misunderstanding of the Bible's teachings. Futurist premillennialists (and I am speaking as one) often make the mistake of assuming that just because most prophecies are yet to be fulfilled, eschatology has nothing to do with the present. As we have already seen, our word "eschatology" comes from two Greek words, *eschaton* (end or last) and *logos* (word, thought, or reason). Strictly speaking, then, eschatology refers to what we think about the end of the world, but we often overlook the fact that the kingdom of God, the age to come, or the new creation (which are all biblical designations for the new reality which will come at the Lord's return) has already arrived in the person and work of Jesus Christ.

We must never forget that the kingdom of God has both a present and future dimension. Despite the fact that the kingdom cannot and will not *fully* arrive until the Lord's return, it is partially here already. Though we would be wrong to claim that the kingdom has been established in this age, we would be absolutely right to claim that the blessings and power of the kingdom are a present possession of those who have accepted the rule of Christ in their lives.

The Mystery of the Kingdom

Needless to say, this dual aspect of the kingdom takes many people by surprise—as it did Jesus' first century disciples. Like the rest of their Jewish contemporaries, they believed that when the Messiah came, He would set up an earthly kingdom. The Old Testament prophets had predicted a restored kingdom through which the whole world would be transformed by the reign of God. So once they were convinced that Jesus was Messiah, it was only natural for the disciples to expect Him to establish His kingdom. That is why James and John tried to beat the rest of the Twelve to the punch by asking Jesus to guarantee them places of honor in His administration (Matt. 20:20–23; Mark 10:35–40). That is also why the disciples had such a hard time understanding or accepting the idea that Jesus would have to die to carry out the Father's will (Mark 8:31–33; 10:32–34; Luke 18:31–34). The Messiah would set up His kingdom, they thought, not die like a criminal on a cross! He cannot be killed; He must transform this age into the glorious age to come.

Jesus *did* preach the coming kingdom. In fact, the Gospel writers often summarized Jesus' message in terms of the kingdom of God: "The time is fulfilled, and the kingdom of God is at hand; repent and believe in the Gospel" (Mark 1:15, NASB; see also Matt. 4:17, 23; Luke 4:43). But Jesus' understanding of the coming kingdom differed markedly from that of His contemporaries. On one occasion the Pharisees asked

Jesus when the kingdom would arrive, and He replied, "The kingdom of God does not come visibly, nor will people say, 'Here it is,' or 'There it is,' because the kingdom of God is within you" (Luke 17:20–21).

Here was a novel idea for the Pharisees and many of their contemporaries: an "invisible" kingdom which people will not be able to locate! Jesus expected to return at the end of the age to defeat the forces of evil and establish the reign of God, but He also expected the kingdom—at least in some sense—to be established in the near future.

Jesus called this dual aspect "the mystery of the kingdom" (Mark 4:11). In the New Testament the word "mystery" denotes the revelation of something which has been hidden. Thus the mystery of the kingdom of God is the fact that the kingdom will arrive in some form *before* its complete manifestation at the end of the age. The kingdom has already arrived in our Lord's Person and work, though in a much different form than it will be revealed at His coming. The future kingdom will come as a glorious divine intervention; but the present kingdom has already come quietly, almost inconspicuously. Through Jesus Christ the blessings of the age to come have broken into this age.

Jesus Himself described the characteristics of the present kingdom in a series of parables which are recorded in Matthew 13 and Mark 4. In these Parables of the Kingdom, Christ presented the kingdom in terms of its hiddenness, obscurity, and initial smallness. Instead of blazing across the heavens like lightning (as it will at Christ's second coming), the kingdom of God has entered the world in utter simplicity.

In the Parable of the Sower (Matt. 13:1–23; Mark 4:1–20), Jesus taught that in the present age people are able to accept or reject the kingdom, according to the conditions of their hearts upon hearing the Gospel. People now enter the kingdom voluntarily, so the kingdom will only be a partial success in this age.

In the Parable of the Tares (Matt. 13:24–30, 36–43),

Jesus indicated that the children of the kingdom will continue to "grow" alongside the children of the evil one until the harvest at the end of the age. The remarkable thing about this parable is its teaching that the kingdom of God and the kingdom of Satan will coexist in the present age until the kingdom of God is fully revealed at the end of the age. Jesus' contemporaries naturally assumed that when God's kingdom was established, the power and kingdom of the devil would be totally destroyed. But Jesus showed that it would not. (This is also the point of the Parable of the Net in Matthew 13:47–50.)

In the Parables of the Mustard Seed and the Yeast (Matt. 13:31–33; Mark 4:30–32), Jesus described the inconspicuous way His kingdom would begin in the present age. People in His day expected the kingdom to be established with power and glory, but Jesus said that its beginning would be almost undetectable—like a mustard seed or a tiny bit of yeast in a lump of dough. But the kingdom will not always remain in this humble and unnoticed condition. Like mustard seeds and yeast, the kingdom will one day extend far beyond its meager beginnings. It may start small, but one day it will fill the earth with God's majesty. (Though Jesus often used "leaven" in a bad sense, that clearly was not His meaning here.)

The Evidence of the Kingdom

Much to their surprise, the disciples discovered that the age to come had broken into this age without completely disrupting it. The kingdom of God had come without totally wiping away the kingdom of Satan. Though the Messiah had come, the present age continued. Yet the present age had been transformed for those who accepted the reign of Christ in their lives. They experienced some of the blessings of the future age in the present. This is exactly what John meant when he claimed that Christians already have eternal life (1 John 5:11–12).

Christ's followers discovered that they had become citizens

of the kingdom while they were still living in this evil age. Some day in the future, Jesus will return a second time to establish the kingdom in its fullness, but in the meantime, His followers experience its blessings and power.

The Kingdom

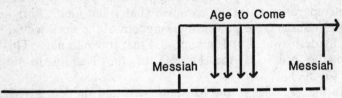

What kind of evidence is there for claiming that the kingdom is here in that form?

1. *The binding of Satan.* One of the main features of Jesus' ministry was His casting out of demons. His power to do so astounded the people around Him (Mark 1:23–28), and even His disciples had the power to exorcise demons in Jesus' name (Mark 6:7; Luke 10:17).

Once the Pharisees accused Jesus of casting out demons by the power of Beelzebub, the prince of demons. Jesus offered another explanation: "Every kingdom divided against itself will be ruined, and every city or household divided against itself will not stand. If Satan drives out Satan, he is divided against himself. How then can his kingdom stand? . . . But if I drive out demons by the Spirit of God, then the kingdom of God has come upon you" (Matt. 12:25–28).

Jesus went on to remind His hearers that no one can rob a strong man's house unless he first binds him (12:29). In Luke's account, the point is made in this way: "When a strong man, fully armed, guards his own house, his possessions are safe. But when someone stronger attacks and overpowers him, he takes away the armor in which the man trusted and divides up the spoils" (Luke 11:21–22).

What is the meaning of Jesus' power over demons? Before

the eschatological defeat and destruction of Satan (Rev. 20:1–10), Jesus has invaded the devil's realm in order to deal him a preliminary but powerful defeat. Of course, this is hardly the end of the story. Satan still has considerable power in the world, but he must give way to the power of the kingdom as demonstrated by Jesus and His followers. All Christians have this same power available to them; they have freedom from the devil's control. Power over Satan is one undeniable proof of the presence of the kingdom, for as Jesus said, "If I drive out demons by the finger of God, then the kingdom of God has come to you" (Luke 11:20).

2. *The gift of salvation.* As we've already seen, redemption and judgment are closely associated with the end of the age. In this sense they are eschatological. However, for those in Christ, salvation is a present reality and the final judgment has already taken place.

Paul made that clear in the Book of Romans. He spoke of "justification" in the past tense: "Since we have been justified through faith, we have peace with God through our Lord Jesus Christ" (5:1). Justification is a legal term which refers to acquittal. To be justified before God means to be declared "not guilty" because of what Christ has done for you. One would not normally expect the verdict before the trial (in this case, the last judgment), but that is precisely what has happened. God has already judged the case of those who accept Christ so that they are no longer in legal jeopardy. "There is therefore now no condemnation for those who are in Christ Jesus" (Rom. 8:1, NASB).

The present experience of salvation is another proof of the present kingdom. Christians have eternal life *now.* Salvation is a present possession. Christians have already been tried and found not guilty before the divine bar of justice because of faith in Jesus Christ.

3. *The guarantee of the Spirit.* In Old Testament prophecy, the outpouring of the Spirit is closely associated with the final Day of the Lord. After discussing the horrible aspects of that Day, the prophet Joel added, "And it shall come to pass

afterward, that I will pour out My Spirit on all flesh" (Joel 2:28, KJV). On the Day of Pentecost Peter informed the curious crowd that "this is what was spoken of through the prophet Joel" (Acts 2:16, NASB). The outpouring of the Spirit, which rightly belonged to the age to come, had occurred in this age. Paul even defines a Christian as one who has the Spirit (Rom. 6) and calls entrance into the body of Christ the "baptism of the Spirit" (1 Cor. 12:13). In Ephesians, Paul refers to the Spirit as a "deposit guaranteeing our inheritance until the redemption of those who are God's possession" (1:14). The Spirit is God's pledge that He will complete the work which He has already begun, that the present kingdom will someday be changed into the glorious, completed one, and that the promises made in this age will be totally kept in the age to come.

4. *The enthronement and reign of Jesus Christ.* After the ascension of Jesus, the disciples undoubtedly were asked: "If Jesus is Messiah, where is His throne?" It was a legitimate question. The kingdom is here, so where is the King?

Many Christians seem to be bothered by the same question. To hear them talk, one would think that Jesus is sitting around, just waiting for the chance to be king. But nothing could be further from the truth. Jesus is already reigning. Paul made this clear in two passages: "Then comes the end, when He delivers up the kingdom to the God and Father, when He has abolished all rule and all authority and power. For He must reign until He has put all His enemies under His feet" (1 Cor. 15:24–25, NASB). Jesus' reign will not begin *after* His enemies are overthrown. Paul said that He will reign *until* His enemies are destroyed. This means that Christ is already reigning: God "raised Him from the dead and seated Him at His right hand in the heavenly realms, far above all rule and authority, power and dominion, and every title that can be given, not only in the present age but also in the one to come. And God placed all things under His feet and appointed Him to be head over everything for the church" (Eph. 1:20–22).

Our Lord reigns. His rule may be hidden at present to those

who don't believe, but someday it will be revealed for all to see. What does all this mean? Only that Christians don't have to wait to experience the reign of Christ. We have already experienced the glories of the kingdom, even if only in a partial sense. The world must wait for the revelation of God's glory, but we don't. For them, the kingdom of God is totally future, but for us, it is present as well.

How does this relate to the charge that premillennialists don't care about the present? It shows that we must be both present- and future-minded. God has not turned His back on this age. He has invaded it. He placed His kingdom here so that His people can experience its blessings. And He called us to be the light of the world and the salt of the earth (Matt. 5:13–16). We also are called Christ's ambassadors (2 Cor. 5:20).

If we have neglected our present responsibilities, it may be because we haven't rightly understood the presence of the kingdom. We haven't used the power available to us: what the whole world will someday be forced to acknowledge, we have as a present possession. We know, though in part, what God will do and what He expects of citizens of His kingdom. If we fail to act like citizens of God's realm, then we are failing to live up to our Lord's expectations for us.

9

Now--Not Yet

Some premillennial Christians don't seem to worry very much about making their behavior match their beliefs. It's not that they don't try to live like Christians; it's just that they have a hard time figuring out how they ought to live in the light of their beliefs about the second coming of Jesus Christ.

In the last chapter we noted two common charges against premillennialists (inconsistency and caring more about the future than the present) and suggested that part of the problem might stem from a faulty view of the kingdom of God. If people realized that the kingdom has both a present and a future dimension, they might take a completely different view of their responsibilities in the world.

Now it's time to face that issue head on. How should Christians shape their present lives in light of the future coming of Jesus Christ?

The Difficulty of the Task

From the outset we have to be perfectly honest: this is not going to be easy, mainly because there seems to be a built-in tension in the Bible when it comes to living in the shadow of the Second Coming. On the one hand, we are told, "Keep watch, because you do not know on what day your Lord will

92

come" (Matt. 24:42). And on the other, Jesus commanded us, "Occupy till I come" (Luke 19:13, KJV).

If we knew exactly when Jesus was going to return, things would be cut and dried. With a definite date for the Second Coming, we could properly arrange our affairs, get our accounts in order, and make the necessary adjustments in our lives. But without such a fixed timetable, we find ourselves in the position of having to be ready *all the time*.

In other words, according to scriptural guidelines, we must constantly be ready for the return of Christ but also be ready in case His coming is delayed. The tension is between "now" (Jesus may come soon) and "not yet" (Jesus may not come for years, maybe not even during our lifetime). This natural tension is even more magnified among pretribulational premillennialists who believe that Jesus *may* come at any moment.

When we know what we're looking for, we can see this built-in tension all around us. And we can understand how people could label our (sometimes unsuccessful) attempts to maintain the biblical balance between "now/not yet" as inconsistency. The late evangelist D. L. Moody related how his whole perspective changed after he became a premillennialist: "The moment a man takes hold of the truth that Jesus Christ is coming back again . . . this world loses its hold upon him; gas stocks and water stocks, and stocks in banks and in horse-railroads are of very much less consequence to him then." But while the possibility of the imminent coming of Christ moved Moody to let go of many earthly entanglements, it did not keep him from founding two educational institutions in Massachusetts (Northfield Seminary for girls and Mount Hermon School for boys), and lending his support to the establishment of a Bible institute in Chicago which eventually took his name.

Probably no better illustration for the now/not yet tension we all feel as premillennialists can be found than the Moody Bible Institute, the great Bible school which has served the evangelical church so well since the 1880s. By the turn of the century, it became a center for the teaching of dispensational premillennialism. The students were being taught that Jesus may return at any moment to rapture the church, yet the administration was busy raising endowment funds so that the same message could be taught for generations to come—in case Christ did not come immediately.

James M. Gray, Moody Bible Institute's able president and a leading premillennialist spokesman in the early 20th century, led the Institute through an amazing building program. From 1904 to 1931, the Institute increased its budget from $376,000 to almost $6 million, its buildings from 8 to 37, its staff from 42 to 280, and its total student body (day, evening, and correspondence) from 1,100 to 17,200.

Those dedicated dispensational premillennialists believed in the possibility of the imminent coming of Christ, but they also knew how to build for the future. In the Institute's magazine (which was then called *The Christian Worker's Magazine*, but has since changed its name to the *Moody Monthly*) an article about the imminent rapture of the church might face an advertisement inviting readers to invest in Moody Bible Institute Annuities to insure a safe and secure retirement.

We have pointed out these matters not to accuse the brethren at the Institute of inconsistency, but to show that they were being absolutely consistent with the biblical teaching of now/not yet.

The Dangers of Imbalance

That doesn't mean that we always keep the built-in tension in perfect balance. Most of us tend to stress one side over the other.

When I was in seminary, I knew some fellow students who put all their emphasis on the *now* side of the tension. They were deeply troubled about the advisability of spending three years of their life studying Greek, Hebrew, systematic theology, New Testament, Old Testament, and church history when Jesus may return at any moment. "There may not be much time left," they reasoned, "so shouldn't we leave school and spend our time in evangelizing the lost?"

Some of those students left school, deciding that it was better to plunge into some form of ministry now than prepare for a future ministry which might never take place because of the Rapture. Now, years later, those former students are probably wondering if they did the right thing. Those of us who remained and finished our seminary preparation are in the ministry and are much better prepared to serve the Lord than those who left. Certainly such decisions are never absolutely clear-cut, but in this case, I believe, the students who left seminary made the wrong decision, even if they made it for all the right reasons.

The lesson to be learned from all this is that we dare not act as though Christ *will* come in the near future when all the Bible teaches is that we should be ready in case He does. Those who put all their eggs in the "now basket" frequently end up looking like fools or fanatics and bring discredit to the doctrine of our Lord's second coming.

We simply have to consider the possibility that we may be here for a while and make our plans accordingly. Any way we look at it, we had better keep the future in mind as we live in the present—just in case we have to live in it! Those who do not maintain such a balance deserve the charge that they are distorting the biblical balance between now/not yet.

Other premillennialists err too much in the other direction. Some of us live as though there were no possibility of Christ's second coming in the near future. We build, save, plan, and conduct our lives as though we had all the time in the world. Practically speaking, the reality of the Lord's return plays no effective role in the way we run our present lives.

Premillennialists who give no thought to Christ's return in their daily lives are most vulnerable to the charges of inconsistency. Posttribulationists, for example, who don't expect Christ at any moment might be tempted to neglect the practical application of His coming to their present lives.

But they are not the only kinds of premillennialists who fail from time to time to live in the light of the Second Coming. We all know people like that. In fact, most of us probably tend to lean in that direction when we fail to keep the biblical balance. It's naturally much easier than constantly trying to be ready. Even pretribulationists recognize that while they may expect Jesus momentarily, there are bills to pay, families to raise, educations to acquire, and retirements to plan for. Despite our firm convictions about eschatology, we still obtain 30-year mortgages, buy life insurance, and pay into pension plans at work. There's nothing wrong with that, except that in our planning for the future, we often forget that how we prepare for the future now should reflect what we think the future will be like.

If we accummulate things, make them the most important objects in our lives, and live like the rest of the world which has no conception of Christ's coming, then we are storing up for ourselves "treasures upon earth, where moth and rust destroy, and where thieves break in and steal" (Matt. 6:19, NASB).

Because we know what God intends to do in the future and how we fit into His plan, we should live in the present with a certain "responsible recklessness." We do not have to worry about the same things (at least not in the same way or to the same degree) as everyone else. Our priorities and commitments lie in other directions. We should live our lives in the full realization that we play an indispensable part in the redemptive plan of God and recognize that our status carries certain demands with it. Our actions will be judged against the measure of the kingdom.

Remember what Jesus said: "If anyone would come after Me, he must deny himself and take up his cross and follow Me. For whoever wants to save his life will lose it, but whoever loses his life for Me will find it. What good will it be for a man if he gains the whole world, yet forfeits his soul? Or what can a man give in exchange for his soul? For the Son of Man is going to come in His Father's glory with His angels, and then He will reward each person according to what he has done" (Matt. 16:24–27). Of all people, we who know about the Lord's second advent should not be hanging on to

NOW—NOT YET / 97

earthly things as though to lose them would be to lose everything. There's more; and God has let us in on His wonderful secret.

This, of course, doesn't mean that we forget about the needs of earthly life, as we shall see in the next three chapters. But it does mean that we should be careful about living as though earthly things were the only future we have. Just as we can't afford to live too much in the "now," we can't make the equally serious mistake of living too much in the "not yet."

Keeping the Biblical Balance

How then can we maintain the delicate balance between being watchful for the Second Coming and being ready for the long haul?

Unfortunately, there are no easy formulas. But there are a few guidelines which may prove helpful.

1. *Our View of the Kingdom.* As we discussed in the last chapter, it is essential that we understand that we don't have to wait until Christ's glorious return to experience some of the blessings and power of the age to come. Through faith in Jesus Christ, God has made the kingdom a present (though partial) possession for those who accept the rule of Christ in their lives. This present experience of the eschatological kingdom puts us in a unique position in the world: we alone have the obligation and opportunity to show the rest of the world a glimpse of what the future kingdom of God will be like. The will of God is not done on earth as it is in heaven, but the world should be able to see a sample of the will of God being carried out in the church.

If we maintain that kind of perspective on the kingdom and our present relation to it, then we will always live in light of the future coming of Christ.

2. *Our Need of Mutual Accountability in the Church.* All people, including Christians, have an almost unlimited capacity for self-deception. We all are occasionally master rationalizers who try to put the best construction on our actions. If there is a way to justify inconsistent or nonbiblical behavior,

we can usually find it. However, it is much more difficult to get away with this kind of thing in a close-knit church fellowship which has learned to speak "the truth in love" (Eph. 4:15).

Paul provides us with a perfect example of how accountability in the church can save us from perpetuating an imbalance in the now/not yet tension. The Thessalonian church had been especially troubled about the Second Coming. In his first letter to the Christians there, Paul had informed them about the rapture of the church (1 Thes. 4), but they had become confused about its timing, with some of the saints assuming that it was so close as to be imminent (2 Thes. 2). A by-product of this erroneous information was a tendency among some of them to stop working in anticipation of Christ's arrival (2 Thes. 3:6–13). These people were not only relying on others within the church to clothe and feed them, but their idleness had also turned them into troublesome busybodies. (We may consider this the first known case of Christians putting too much emphasis on the now side of the tension.)

What was Paul's suggested solution? " 'If a man will not work, he shall not eat.' . . . In the name of the Lord Jesus Christ, we command and urge such people to settle down and earn the bread they eat. . . . If anyone does not obey our instruction in this letter, take special note of him. Do not associate with him, in order that he may feel ashamed" (2 Thes. 3:10, 12, 14).

One of the biggest scandals of modern church life is the lack of discipline and willingness to correct an erring brother or sister. In this particular case, Paul gave strict instructions: let the people in question know that their behavior is improper in light of biblical eschatology and restrict Christian fellowship until the error is corrected. If we were to apply that piece of advice literally in our current situation, I fear that our churches would be emptied almost immediately.

Fortunately, that kind of extreme action is not necessary in most cases because the offense against the biblical balance isn't that obvious. However, we would all benefit greatly by a local body of believers which was aware of the biblical tension between the now/not yet and constantly evaluated how its members were maintaining it. What I might overlook in my own life, a fellow Christian might easily detect. But naturally, that would take a special kind of fellowship and a special kind of commitment to being truly biblical in our daily lives. It's difficult, but it can be done.

3. *An Awareness of the World around Us.* Not only do we need to keep each other honest in the church, but we also need to understand the world around us. We'll never be able to avoid compromise with the world's standards unless we more fully comprehend how exactly the world seeks to force us into its own mold. And we'll never be able to effectively respond to the world's needs unless we know what they are.

General George S. Patton, the brilliant American tank commander in World War II, was able to deal the German forces a decisive defeat in North Africa because he had read the German commander's textbooks on military strategy and tank warfare. He knew what he had to do because he knew exactly what his enemy was going to do. In much the same way, we Christians have an obligation to know the world in which we live. We already have a huge head start because we know where the world is going and what will happen to it according to God's plan. Knowing God's purposes, we can effectively gauge our behavior to reflect them: we can avoid fruitless entanglements with the world which we know will lead nowhere; and we can take action to live out the demands of the kingdom of Christ's ambassadors in the world.

In other words, when we know the world as we should, we are prepared to take both defensive and offensive action. In the remaining three chapters, we will examine some specific suggestions as to how we can live out the biblical balance we have been discussing. We will look into three areas: personal life-style, evangelism, and concern for those outside the body of Christ.

10

Living as Though We Really Mean It

"Dear friends, now we are children of God, and what we will be has not yet been made known. But we know that when He appears, we shall be like Him, for we shall see Him as He is. Everyone who has this hope in him purifies himself, just as He is pure" (1 John 3:2–3).

Our knowledge of biblical eschatology should have a profound effect on our personal lives. Because God has let us in on His future plans, we must readjust our present lives accordingly.

As we saw in the last chapter, that is often easier said than done. Our lives must be lived in a state of tension between being ready for the Second Coming and being prepared for the long haul in case our Lord doesn't return in the near future. Keeping this biblical balance is a difficult business, and most of us have to be on our guard so that we don't veer toward one side or the other.

In chapter 8 we noted that a recurring criticism against premillennialists is that they do not act all that differently from other kinds of Christians. Apart from teaching their particular beliefs about the Second Coming and buying an enormous number of books on eschatology, their Christian lives are indistinguishable from other believers who don't share their prophetic views. In a way, that observation is absolutely correct: when premillennialists keep the now and not yet in their proper proportions, they will be fairly inconspicuous. It's only when we go off the deep end by acting as though the present were the only thing worth worrying about, or living as though we have all the time in the world, that a large gap appears between our profession and our practice.

A Distinctive Premillennial Life-Style?

At times we premillennialists sound as if we have cornered the market on Christian virtue. We all but claim that it is impossible to live the Christian life without a correct understanding of biblical eschatology. One prominent premillennialist pastor in the early 1900s claimed that the premillennialists in his church were always the best students of the Bible, the most devout, the most consistent pray-ers, the most conscientious givers, and the best personal witnesses. That may have been true in his church, but it would be pretty hard to make any sweeping generalizations about all premillennialists.

When we come right down to it, all Christians, no matter what their eschatology, perceive the Christian life in pretty much the same way. Thus when premillennialist leaders call on their fellow believers to live in the light of Christ's return, they end up sounding like everyone else.

Reuben A. Torrey, world evangelist and Christian educator at the Moody Bible Institute and at the Bible Institute of Los Angeles at the turn of the century, urged people to prepare for the Second Coming by "separation from the world's indulgences of the flesh, from the world's immersion in the affairs of this life and intense daily earnestness in prayer." Another premillennialist gave pretty much the same advice: we should show our readiness for the Lord's return by "teaching, testifying, giving, sacrificing, suffering, using mind, hands, feet, whatever we have, and whatever we can for His honor and for making Him and His will known among men for their welfare."

That is sound advice, but there is nothing in it to which a postmillennialist or an amillennialist could not say a hearty

"Amen!" No matter what we believe about the Second Coming, there are certain basics in living for Christ which all believers recognize and try to follow.

Do Premillennialists Have a Better Idea?

That doesn't mean, however, that our eschatological beliefs do not have a direct bearing on our life-styles. I have found that while premillennialism does not lead to a distinctive life-style, it often affects the reasons we give for our actions.

Historically (or at least in the American context) premillenialists have often used their doctrine of the possibility of the any-moment rapture of the church as a means for regulating personal behavior. Obviously, dispensational premillennialists who believe in a pretribulational Rapture are the main practitioners of this approach, but most (if not all) premillennialists have come across it at one time or another.

Specifically, it works like this: When we find ourselves in a questionable situation or on the verge of giving in to some sinful temptation, the possibility of Jesus' immediate return acts as a deterrent. We find ourselves asking, "Would I want to be doing *that* when Jesus comes?" Anyone who has read much premillennialist literature or heard many sermons on the imminent Second Coming has encountered that question in one form or another countless times.

Robert Speer, long-time secretary of the Presbyterian foreign missions board, put it as well as anyone when he said, "No man can easily do an unclean and unholy thing expecting at that moment that Jesus may come. Can I cross the threshold of the questionable place? Can I read the questionable book? Can I be found with that questionable story on my lips? Can I be on the verge of that sin, if I am expecting that at that very moment Jesus Christ may come?"

Reuben A. Torrey devised a rule of thumb which could be applied in any situation: "Do not do anything that you would not be glad to have your Lord find you doing if He should come. . . . Never go anywhere that you would not like to have the Lord find you if He should come."

Anyone who seriously considers the possibility of being "caught in the act" by the returning Christ will clean up his life considerably.

One evangelist told the story of two church members who were taking a walk along the streets of New York City just before the turn of the century. As they passed through the theater district, one remarked that a certain play had received rave notices and asked if the other wanted to buy a ticket.

"No," the second church member replied, "I don't want to." When asked why not, he explained, "The Lord might come while I was in there, and I wouldn't want Him to find me in such a place."

Now you might not think that being in a theater when the trumpet blows would be such an embarrassing predicament, but this brother did—and his belief in the possibility of Christ's coming at any time was enough to keep him from going in and taking the chance.

Abuses

All this may sound utterly ridiculous to nonpremillennialists (or nondispensational premillennialists) who do not think in terms of an any-moment arrival of Jesus Christ. But anyone who has been reared under this kind of teaching knows the tremendous power it has to shape and regulate behavior. God only knows how many sins were never committed, or borderline activities avoided, because Jesus might return and catch us red-handed.

Anything that powerful has the potential to be abused; and this doctrine has been mishandled from time to time.

Probably the biggest abuse occurs in the area of instilling an unbiblical attitude of fear and intimidation into the minds of some people—especially the very young. I don't remember who was responsible, but somewhere along the line I picked up the erroneous idea that bad little boys (even those who had accepted Jesus as Saviour) might be left behind at the rapture of the church. I might have been devious and a bit too much to handle from time to time, but I wasn't stupid. I did not want to be around to face Antichrist and the Tribulation without the rest of my family. I can still vividly remember coming home from school when I was about 10 years old and, upon finding my mother unexpectedly gone, coming to the terrifying conclusion that I'd been left behind. From talking with others and the reading I've done, I'm certain that my experience is not that unusual.

That kind of thing is a terrible distortion of the Bible's teaching on the Second Coming. It puts the glorious appearing of Jesus Christ on the same level as the bogeyman and Santa's helpers who patrol the world to discover who deserves Christmas presents and who doesn't. No wonder some people within the church develop a "Second Coming phobia" which causes them to prefer a return of the Black Plague to the *Parousia* of their Lord! When we get to the point where we primarily appreciate the Second Coming for its deterrent value, then we had better take another look at Scripture. According to Paul, we should long for Christ's appearing (2 Tim. 4:8), not view it as a dreaded cosmic "candid camera" which might surprise us when we least expect it.

In addition to using this doctrine to create unnecessary anxiety, some believers have found it helpful when perpetuating their own kinds of legalism. As we all know, it is possible to create guilt when there shouldn't be any. One of evangelicalism's besetting sins has been the tendency to equate certain kinds of behavior (or lack of behavior) with the proper Christian life, even when the biblical justification for such standards is a bit sketchy.

We often miss the rather obvious fact that in our churches we judge a person's orthodoxy by what he believes and how he acts. Believing the right things is not enough; a person must also live up to whatever standard of Christian living that particular body of believers has determined is truly biblical. Fortunately, most of us manage to keep pretty close to Scripture in these practical matters, but sometimes we have a hard time telling the difference between what the Bible actually says and what we have been taught to believe it says. The result is that we are often dogmatic concerning certain areas of behavior about which the Bible has little or nothing to say.

Since the Bible might not be very clear, some Christians obtain strict conformity on a particular issue by instilling legalistic guilt among those who might question the accepted interpretation. The doctrine of the Second Coming can be used in such circumstances to keep the wavering on the straight and narrow.

By bringing up the "threat" of Christ's return, such legalists have at their disposal an effective tool to keep everybody in line. The most tragic thing about this abuse of the doctrine of the Second Coming is that it keeps people from really digging into the Scripture for answers to the issues under discussion. As long as people feel guilty and fear the Lord's return, they do not have the freedom to explore the Word.

Fortunately, this abuse might not be as prevalent as the first; but when it does appear, we should recognize it for what it is—a distortion of the belief in the Second Coming in an attempt to perpetuate and force on others one's own lifestyle.

We must not let such misunderstandings gain the upper hand, because they produce a shallow Christian discipleship. God is not only concerned about *what* we do; He pays special attention to *why* we do what we do. Men judge us by our outward actions; but God looks at our motives. Are we living holy lives because of our love for God and our desire to please Him, or are we toeing the line because we don't want to be embarrassed or surprised at Christ's coming? One approach marks true Christian discipleship, while the other is the action of those who fear the Lord they are supposed to be following willingly.

Do we suppose that Christ is not always with us and does not always see what we do? We don't have to wait for the Second Coming to be accountable for our actions.

Another Approach
All we've said so far has applied primarily to dispensationalists.

Because they believe that the Rapture may occur at any moment, they most naturally would be concerned about Christ breaking in unexpectedly on their current activities. But dispensationalists are not the only premillennialists whose lives are (or should be) affected by their eschatology.

At first glance, posttribulational premillennialists (those who expect the Rapture after the Tribulation) seem to have an insurmountable problem. How can they obey the command to "watch" when they deny the possibility that Christ may appear momentarily? Watchfulness, pretribulationists insist, requires the doctrine of the imminent Rapture.

Posttribulationists, however, deny that the Bible teaches the kind of "watchfulness" advocated by dispensationalists. They point out that there are a number of Greek words which are translated "watch" and that those which imply watching in terms of looking for something or riveting one's attention on something expected (*tereo* and *paratereo*) are never used in conjunction with the Second Coming (Matt. 27:36, 54; Mark 3:2; Luke 6:7; Acts 9:24).

Furthermore they show that another word which is translated in the King James Version as "watch" in 1 Peter 4:7 (*nepho*), actually means "to be sober," which is how more recent versions put it.

More important to their linguistic argument, however, is the posttribulationists' demonstration that the words which do refer to our attitude in the light of Christ's coming (*gregoreo* and *agrupneo*) mean primarily "to be sleepless," "to be awake," or even "to be alert and vigilant." Most of the time, these words are used to refer to spiritual vigilance in the face of trial or tribulation (Matt. 26:38; Acts 20:31; 1 Cor. 16:13; Eph. 6:18; Col. 4:2; Heb. 13:17). So when the words are applied to the Second Coming, "keep on the alert," (Mark 13:33; Luke 21:36, NASB), they should carry the same meaning.

In other words, posttribulationists contend that when we are told in the New Testament to "watch" for the Second Coming, we are actually being urged to keep spiritually alert and vigilant, not look for the returning Christ like a hostess who isn't sure when her dinner guests will arrive, and keeps looking out the front window to see if they're in sight.

This seems to be a valid conclusion. The New Testament doesn't claim that the Second Coming should catch believers unprepared. Even though we do not know the exact time, we have enough information not to be taken by surprise. After informing the Thessalonians that certain things must come to pass before the Lord's return, Paul added:

> Now, brothers, about times and dates we do not need to write to you, for you know very well that the Day of the Lord will come like a thief in the night. While people are saying, 'Peace and safety,' destruction will come on them suddenly, as labor pains on a pregnant woman, and they will not escape. But you, brothers, are not in darkness so that this day should surprise you like a thief. You are all sons of the light and sons of the day. We do not belong to the night or to the darkness. So then, let us not be like others who are asleep, but let us be alert [*gregoreo*] and self-controlled [*nepho*] (1 Thes. 5:1–6).

Jesus gave similar practical advice following His Olivet Discourse. He warned believers about the coming events at the end of the age and then urged them to be watchful, and thus keep the Second Coming from being unexpected, not because it is unexpected (Matt. 24:36–44; Mark 13:32–37; Luke 21:34–36).

Some Biblical Guidelines

What practical suggestions can we make for those who really want to live consistently with the doctrine of the Second Coming?

1. *Watchfulness*. As we have just seen, this will mean different things, depending on one's form of premillennialism. Pretribulationists will attempt to be watchful because the Rapture may occur at any moment, and posttribulationists will keep watch because they don't want the events of the future,

leading to the Second Coming, to slip by them unawares.

But both positions can learn something from the other. Both sides would agree that biblical watchfulness means more than just pressing one's nose against the window pane in anticipation of the Lord's return. It means aggressive discipleship, a rigorous application of the whole counsel of God to daily life, and an eagerness to seek first the kingdom of God and His righteousness (Matt. 6:33).

Those who truly watch for the Lord's return will not live as though He were not coming at all. As we come to understand more fully how the Second Coming fits into God's overall redemptive plans, our lives should increasingly conform to His purpose for us—and that means being alert, vigilant, and watchful as God's will is worked out in the world. "So then, let us not be like others who are asleep, but let us be alert and self-controlled" (1 Thes. 5:6).

2. *Steadfastness.* In the Apostle John's letters to the seven churches (Rev. 2—3), the saints are instructed to endure. At the conclusion of each message, a promise is given to those who overcome.

The Christian life is no joy ride to glory. There are dangers along the way. In what must rank as a classic understatement, the Apostle Paul, after being in constant danger on his first missionary journey, observed, " 'We must go through many hardships to enter the kingdom of God' " (Acts 14:22).

But along with the inevitable challenges of the Christian life come the promises of victory in the end. Our Lord said, "I have told you these things so that in Me you may have peace. In this world you will have trouble. But take heart! I have overcome the world" (John 16:33). God has not left us to fight our battles alone. He has outfitted us with His own armor so that there will be no question of our ultimate victory (Eph. 6:10–18).

Probably the single most important reason why God told us of His eschatological plans is that when we know how things will work out, we will be able to stand fast when troubles come.

3. *Moral Purity.* In addition to standing firm against the

attacks of the evil one, Christians must demonstrate lives of unimpeachable purity in light of the Second Coming. This is the message of 1 John 3:2–3.

Christians usually equate purity with separation from the world. "Do not love the world or anything in the world. If anyone loves the world, the love of the Father is not in him" (1 John 2:15).

But separation from the world does not mean withdrawal from it. After Paul advised the Corinthian church to put an unrepentant erring brother out of the fellowship, he reminded the church that he was not advocating total separation from "the people of the world who are immoral, or the greedy and swindlers, or idolaters. In that case you would have to leave this world" (1 Cor. 5:10).

Purity means more than just physical separation from the world, and separation from the world means more than cutting off ties with evil people around us. Jesus should be our model here. He maintained total faithfulness to the Father while He openly associated with some of the most notorious characters of His day. " 'It is not the healthy who need a doctor, but the sick. I have not come to call the righteous, but sinners' " (Mark 2:17).

Many of us pat ourselves on the back because we maintain a strict separation from the world in external matters, but internally adopt the world's values and outlook. It is easier to steer clear of some of the blatantly immoral activities in the world than it is to avoid becoming ensnared in the world's materialism, self-centeredness, and striving for personal power and status.

No one who takes the Second Coming seriously can dare neglect a holy life. "Therefore put on the full armor of God, so that when the day of evil comes, you may be able to stand your ground, and after you have done everything, to stand" (Eph. 6:13).

4. *Firm Allegiance to the Corporate Body of Christ.* In many of the discussions of biblical eschatology, the importance of the body of Christ in the prophetic story is almost totally

ignored.

In his great letter on the church, Paul argued that God's ultimate aim in redemption is "to bring all things in heaven and earth together under one head, even Christ" (Eph. 1:10). For Paul, the significance of the church is that it is currently the only visible evidence that the unification process has already begun. That Christ has broken down the barrier separating Jew and Gentile and formed them into "one new man" is proof positive that God has started bringing the universe under Christ's control (2:11–22).

The existence of the Christian church thus has eschatological significance: it is a present sign of what someday will extend through the entire created order. How then can those interested in eschatology neglect the church? How can they think it possible to "free lance" or live as solitary Christians outside of a fellowship of believers? Those who thus neglect the corporate body of Christ are actually placing themselves outside and against God's redemptive purposes.

Those who really believe in the Second Coming will try to live like it. They will incorporate into their personal lifestyles evidence that Jesus is coming again. But we who take eschatology seriously also have an obligation to the unsaved world around us. In the next chapter we will see how believing in the return of Jesus Christ should affect our commitment to evangelization and world missions.

11

Spreading the Word

There is one thing critics have never been able to pin on premillennialists: that they neglect evangelism and world missions. The truth is that premillennialists have always considered spreading the Gospel to be their primary God-given responsibility. As we shall see in the next chapter, sometimes our concern for evangelism has made us overlook some of our other duties, but as a group (there are always individual exceptions) premillennialists have never ignored God's command to go into all the world and preach the Gospel.

Leaders in Evangelism

Some people might even call premillennialists the champions of evangelistic work. One undeniable fact of American church history is that for the last hundred years, all leading revivalists who have gained national recognition have been confirmed premillennialists.

For much of the 19th century, a majority of American evangelicals were postmillennialists, including Charles G. Finney, the leading revivalist of the early 19th century. Postmillennialism and revivalism seemed to go together. If the church is charged with bringing in the Millennium through the gradual Christianization of the world, then vast numbers of conversions were needed. Finney and his followers therefore developed various revival techniques which all but guaranteed, they promised, a revival anytime and anyplace believers were willing to pay the price in hard work and fervent prayer.

As a result, postmillennialists became aggressive evangelists. They had tremendous motivation: a combination of a concern for souls and a commitment to bring in the earthly kingdom of God.

By the time of the American Civil War, the evangelical churches had grown in such numbers and prestige that historians of the period often speak of the United States as an "evangelical empire" during those years. They don't mean to imply that most Americans were confirmed evangelical believers, only that the evangelical churches exerted the most powerful influence within the American culture. In many ways, the mid-nineteenth century was the "golden age" of American evangelical Christianity.

But at the height of evangelical influence, something began to go wrong. A bloody civil war divided the country and the churches. Immigrants in unprecedented numbers flooded the cities, leaving many people wondering whether American ideals could last much longer. Pent-up social tensions broke out in numerous and frighteningly violent strikes and even pitched battles between workers and federal troops. Cities were fast becoming pestholes of unsanitary living conditions, crime, vice of every description, and overpopulation.

To make matters worse, the churches which had recently seemed invincible were now declining in membership and influence and many congregations fled the cities, leaving no resident evangelical witness among the swarming immigrants. Many of those who wanted to maintain their Christian convictions under these difficult circumstances were finding it increasingly difficult to do so, given the rise of such things as the theory of evolution and biblical higher criticism which undermined traditional evangelical doctrines.

Postmillennialists suddenly found it very difficult to convince anyone that the Millennium was just around the corner.

Many evangelicals began to shop around for an eschatological perspective that could better explain things as they really were. They found that premillennialism could account for the world's apparent decline as part of God's plan for the ages, yet still hold out the promise of Christ's eventual victory over all the enemies of God.

Many revivalists who had been laboring under postmillennialism's promise of a soon-drawing Millennium immediately saw in premillennialism a new, even more powerful stimulus to evangelism.

D. L. Moody, who became a premillennialist in the late 1860s or early 1870s, claimed that his new eschatology increased his desire to win the lost: "I have felt like working three times as hard ever since I came to understand that my Lord was coming back again."

J. Wilbur Chapman, one of Moody's fellow revivalists, testified that premillennialism "has been one of the never-failing inspirations in my ministry. It has constantly stirred me on to increased activity in connection with my evangelistic work, and but for the blessed hope, I think that many times I would have grown discouraged and felt like giving everything up."

What was there about premillennialism which drove Moody on to more zeal and kept Chapman going during times of discouragement? Its teaching about the nearness of Christ's return introduced a new note of urgency into evangelism. If the premillennialists who predict an any-moment Rapture of the church are correct, many revivalists reasoned, then there is no time to lose. Postmillennialists might have the luxury of believing that Christ's coming would wait for the completion of the missionary efforts, but premillennialists had no such assurances. According to their reading of the Bible, the church was not intended to convert the world, but God did hold it accountable for spreading the Gospel throughout the world until Jesus comes.

That premillennialists never expected to Christianize the world might seem a bit discouraging, but the doctrine was, in fact, an enormous spur to activity. Time is short. Tomorrow may be too late. Save as many as you can in the time that you have.

As Moody himself put it, "I look on this world as a wrecked vessel. God has given me a lifeboat, and said to me, 'Moody, save all you can.'"

History shows that Moody did, and that every major American revivalist after him shared his premillennial views and credited them with motivating them to save the lost and win as many as possible before Jesus returns. Reuben A. Torrey, Sam P. Jones, Billy Sunday, and Billy Graham—premillennialists all!

A New Reason (and Way) to Bring Them In

Premillennialism provided revivalists and lay Christians who witnessed to their friends with more than a new sense of urgency. It gave them a new tool, a new reason to get people to make their decision for Christ.

In general, premillennialism is a powerful catalyst to conversion. Once a person is made fully aware of what lies in store for the world, he may want to align himself with Christ, who will someday return and dispose of the Antichrist and the devil and all those who preferred them to Him.

Dispensational premillennialism, on the other hand, added another reason for accepting Christ immediately—so that one would not be left behind when Christ comes to rapture His church.

Prior to the development of the doctrine of the pretribulational/any-moment Rapture, revivalists could only warn their audiences that they might unexpectedly die without Christ and thus lose their opportunity to make their decision for Christ. But now sinners had something else to worry about—having to face the horrors of the Great Tribulation when God pours out His wrath on the unbelieving world. Many revivalists rightly concluded that most people wanted to go through the Tribulation about as much as they wanted to go to hell, and they rarely missed a chance to press the point home.

Anyone who takes the time to read the sermons of those

who switched to dispensational premillennialism (or who has attended very many evangelistic services today) knows that alluding to the possibility of being left behind at the rapture of the church became a mainstay in much evangelistic preaching.

Sermons abound with fictionalized stories about what it will be like to discover that the world's Christians have been raptured in anticipation of the revelation of the Antichrist.

The story is told of a man who one night, after reading Paul's passage on the rapture of the church (1 Thes. 4), dreamed that when he woke up the next morning, his wife and children (all devout Christians) were missing. He carefully searched the house but discovered that all the doors and windows were still locked and even his wife's clothes were laid out as they had been the night before.

Still somewhat mystified by their unexplained disappearance, he went to the home of his sister-in-law who lived nearby and discovered that her maid had also left without a trace. After breakfasting on coffee without cream (the milkman had missed his delivery that day), the man went to work where he found part of his staff also absent.

By the end of the day, everyone had put two and two together: Christ had raptured His church during the night. Needless to say, the churches quickly filled, and the pastors who still remained (!) were severely criticized for not properly preparing their congregations for the Rapture; but they said that they had only taught what they had learned in seminary!

At that point in the man's dream, he woke up screaming—who can blame him? Startled by his sudden outburst, his wife —who was thankfully still by his side—asked what was the matter. After stuttering out the contents of his nightmare, the man got right with God.

The power of such a vision has never been lost among premillennialists, especially those of the dispensational variety. Currently, one can find on the shelves of Bible bookstores a whole collection of Christian "novels" which try to describe what it will be like for those whose loved ones have been caught up at the Rapture and who thus have to face the Tribulation alone. At least one of these stories has been made into a feature length movie which has been used in evangelistic services all over the country with great success.

Naturally, nondispensational premillennialists are deprived of such a valuable evangelistic tool. Since they don't believe the Rapture can occur at any time, they can't make use of it in the same way in evangelism. But that doesn't mean that they are any less motivated to spread the Word. They simply stress that those who refuse to ally themselves with the coming King run the risk of facing the wrath of God which will be poured out on the earth during the Tribulation.

Since they do not believe the Bible teaches it, posttribulationists don't teach the obviously more popular idea that the church will escape the Tribulation. All Scripture promises, they say, is that God will somehow protect His people by giving them His mark (Rev. 7) so that they do not experience His wrath, and give them the grace they need to endure the persecution that Antichrist will level against them.

It is not as appealing as the pretribulationist version. Nobody—not even posttribulationists—want to go through that kind of experience.

Faithful Supporters of World Missions

The same reasons which lead some premillennialists to enter evangelism send others into foreign missions. Despite those who argue that the belief that the world will never be won to Christ short of the Second Coming undermines the missionary task, premillennialists have maintained their enthusiastic support of missions when others have fallen by the wayside.

An important reason for premillennialists' concern with the spread of the Gospel around the world is that they see a relationship between world evangelization and the Second Coming: "And this Gospel of the kingdom shall be preached in the whole world for a witness to all nations, and then the end shall come" (Matt. 24:14, NASB).

All premillennialists admit such a relationship, even though they can't agree on what it is. Some premillennialists see this prediction as one of the characteristics of the "last days," the period which stretches from the Incarnation to the signs immediately leading up to the Second Coming. Those who don't believe that there is any prophecy to be fulfilled prior to the Rapture argue that this condition was fulfilled by the Apostles in the first century or will be fulfilled by the believing Jewish remnant in the Tribulation. Still other premillennialists seem to make Christ's coming contingent on the evangelization of the world.

William Bell Riley, a Baptist pastor and educator who became a leader in the fundamentalist movement in the 1920s and 30s, was a dispensationalist who held this view. In one place, Riley sounded as though he believed that the church's faithfulness in evangelizing the world would determine when Jesus returned: "We have something to do with His return! We have something to do with His ascension to the throne. . . . In one sense His crown is in our hands."

That's probably overdoing it, but it does illustrate how important missionary work was to premillennialists. In fact, some of the most dynamic leaders in the evangelical missions movement in the last hundred years have been premillennialists. Hudson Taylor, who founded the China Inland Mission which was at one time the largest mission agency in the world, was a premillennialist. When the Christian and Missionary Alliance was formed in 1887 under the leadership of A. B. Simpson, it adhered to a "fourfold gospel": conversion, entire sanctification, divine healing, and the premillennial Second Coming. Within a very short time the Alliance became a large and effective missionary force and remains today among the leaders of evangelical missions.

A. J. Gordon, a premillennialist Baptist pastor from Boston, founded the Boston Missionary Training School in 1889 for the expressed purpose of providing missionaries for the Congo. The school sent out many missionary candidates and eventually became Gordon College.

We could extend the list almost indefinitely, but you get the point. Those who believe that Jesus is coming again naturally have a concern for spreading the Gospel.

We would be wrong to assume, however, that premillennialism is the *only* or even the *main* reason for wanting to share the Gospel. There are others.

Responding to God's Mandate

First of all, *God commands us to spread the Gospel*. "All authority has been given to Me in heaven and on earth. Go therefore and make disciples of all nations, baptizing them in the name of the Father and the Son and the Holy Spirit, teaching them to observe all that I commanded you; and lo, I am with you always, even to the end of the age" (Matt. 28:18–20, NASB).

Though Jesus includes an eschatological element in His command (His being with us to the end of the age), the primary emphasis is not eschatological. We must spread the Gospel because Jesus is Lord ("All authority has been given to Me in heaven and on earth"). The Lord Jesus deserves to be worshiped, and it's up to those who love Him to declare His Lordship throughout the earth and make disciples.

Second, *God loves the world and desires its salvation*. "For God so loved the world that He gave His one and only Son. that whoever believes in Him shall not perish but have everlasting life" (John 3:16). The reason for the incarnation of Jesus Christ, the Son of God, was the love of God.

Jesus' parables of the lost sheep, lost coin, and lost son (Luke 15) prove that God seeks the lost. God's love is so immense that He is like the shepherd who risks everything to find one lost sheep, or the woman who must tear her house apart until she finds the coin she has misplaced, or the father who, though he has been severely and unjustly wronged, is willing to welcome his lost son home with open arms.

Since God is that kind of a God, He expects those who follow Him to do the same. Sometimes we forget that the second coming of Christ and all that it involves is just one part of God's plan of *salvation*. Jesus will not return primarily to get even with Satan and his supporters. He's coming to save and vindicate His people and finish the redemption process so that they can spend eternity in the new heaven and earth.

Premillennialists must be concerned about spreading the Gospel because of the great love of God for the lost.

Finally, *God has no other way to spread His word.* In His divine providence and omniscience, God has chosen to spread His Gospel through the foolishness of preaching, and has selected us as His agents. "How, then, can they call on the One they have not believed in? And how can they believe in the One of whom they have not heard? And how can they hear without someone preaching to them? And how can they preach unless they are sent?" (Rom. 10:14–15)

No one will come to Christ unless Christians fulfill their obligations to be spreaders of the Word. Modern communications technology has provided us with new ways to relate and transmit the message of Christ to people in our own time. It doesn't really matter how we do it; the important thing is that we act like "Christ's ambassadors, as though God were making His appeal through us" (2 Cor. 5:20).

This is where personal responsibility really comes to bear. People don't have to be professional evangelists or missionaries to share in the spreading of the Gospel. Wherever we are and whatever we do for a living is good enough. Each Christian, as a member of Christ's body, is a part of God's plan for the ages which will be consummated at the Lord's return. A believer is going against God's purpose for him in the world if he neglects evangelism in some form. As a noted Swiss theologian observed, "The church exists by mission as fire exists by burning."

Premillennialism has deepened the commitment to evangelism and world mission within the church and has motivated countless individuals to a more intensive sharing of the Gospel. But has it deepened Christians' commitment to social righteousness and quickened among its adherents the desire to become more actively involved in the world's needs? That's the issue which we will face in the next chapter.

12

Doing Deeds of Righteousness

Premillennialists have labored tirelessly in evangelism, but we have earned poor to failing marks in the area of social justice. We have always been vitally concerned about the existence of personal sin, but seem to have a hard time getting too worked up over the widespread evidence of social unrighteousness all around us.

Historians of American religion frequently claim that premillennialism is at least partially to blame for the decline of evangelical social concern. Premillennialism's pessimistic view of the present and its denial that Christians can do anything to alleviate conditions before the Second Coming have sapped the strength of evangelicals and caused them to turn their backs on the world's needs.

In this chapter we will examine this rather disturbing assertion in detail and attempt to determine what our attitudes should be toward the social problems around us.

The Source of the Problem
In chapter 7 we discovered that the kingdom of God has both a present and a future dimension. Though the kingdom will not be established in its fullness till the return of Jesus Christ, it has been partially established in the present age through

the person and work of Jesus. Through Christ's salvation and the work of the Spirit, Christians have experienced some of the blessings and power of the future kingdom here and now. Those who are in Christ, in other words, live in two ages at the same time.

We also discovered in our discussion of this truth that some premillennialists have neglected or misunderstood the present nature of the kingdom of God. Since the kingdom will not be completely established until the *Parousia,* they assume that it has no real impact on the current age.

With this view they believe that God has turned His back on the world and given it over to the devil until the Second Coming. It's almost as though God has relinquished His sovereignty and let Satan have his own way for the time being. Believers, therefore, are aliens on a hostile planet. They must withdraw from the world as much as possible and have little or nothing to do with it.

The people who accept this view are not necessarily hard-hearted or unconcerned individuals. They base their convictions on what they believe (wrongly, I think) the Bible teaches.

How might a person with this view of the world react to the many social, economic, and political needs in the world today? If he really wanted to be consistent with his basic beliefs about the nature of this age and the Christian's responsibilities in it, he would have to conclude that these needs are the natural result of God letting the devil run things and that believers must not interfere.

We can see this same reaction throughout the history of premillennialism in the United States. As social conditions began to worsen at the end of the 19th century, many premillennialists began to argue along these lines: since the days of King Nebuchadnezzar of Babylon, God has given control of the world to the Satan-inspired Gentile powers (thus we're in the "times of the Gentiles," Luke 21:24). Since these powers have been ordained by God to rule until the Second Coming, the church must not interfere with their operations or try to usurp their authority. Even when these governments are tyrannical and corrupt, Christians have no right to try to change them. In short, believers have no business helping Satan run his world. If he makes a mess of things, he should not expect God's people to run to the rescue.

As one premillennialist expressed it, the church "must not try to help the Christ-rejecting world make a success of its job. It must wait until the world's 'inning' is over, when the church's time will come." After the world has failed miserably to establish peace and prosperity apart from God, Jesus Christ will return, establish His millennial kingdom, and show the world how it's done.

We can imagine what people with this point of view thought of those other Christians who rolled up their sleeves to correct the social injustices in the world! They were naive and playing right into Satan's hands. By reforming the world, they were helping Satan perpetuate the idea that mankind could make it without God. By working to alleviate social unrighteousness, these misguided Christians were preventing people from realizing how terrible and miserable life can be apart from God's rule. Thus by making things better, reformers and do-gooders were actually fighting against God's intention for this age!

One premillennialist went so far as to say that "Satan would have a reformed world, a beautiful world, a moral world, a world of great achievements." Why would Satan, who usually produces misery and chaos, want to reform his world a little? The answer is obvious: to keep people comfortable enough not to see their desperate need for salvation. People who are content don't think they really need God, but those who are miserable are much more willing to consider Him. Thus by making things better, reformers were reducing the numbers of people who might take spiritual things seriously.

Naturally (and fortunately), not all premillennialists ac cepted this rather extreme position. Even those who tended to see the kingdom of God as primarily future did not all share this point of view. But this interpretation did and still does exist.

Biblical Evaluation

The only thing wrong with this position is that it appears to have little or no biblical support. Even though Satan exerts a mighty influence in the present age, God has not given him a blank check to do as he pleases. Neither has He turned His back on the present age. He has established (in a partial and hidden form) His kingdom in this age and is still seeking the lost. God's people are still in this age, and He is intimately concerned with their welfare. Many premillennialists, it seems, give up on the world before God does.

The most serious shortcoming of this point of view is its distortion of God's *present* concern with the issues of social unrighteousness and its virtual denial of the personal righteousness of God. To imply that Almighty God has given Satan *carte blanche* to do as he pleases and to teach Christians not to be involved in moral and spiritual issues (which is what social problems basically are) reflects a serious misreading of the Old and New Testaments.

Since we've been dealing with prophecy throughout this book, let's pay a little closer attention to the prophets. As we search through Old Testament prophecy for predictions about the end times, we often overlook the total context and the original conditions which prompted the prophet's reaction. When we do that needed background work, we discover that God is deeply concerned about social justice and even judges men and nations on the basis of how they treat the poor and oppressed.

When interpreters of prophecy come to the Book of Amos in the Old Testament, they usually restrict their attention to its section on the Day of the Lord (5:16–20). But the rest of the prophecy tells us something immeasurably important about God's righteousness and our responsibilities in the present age.

Though he was a citizen of Judah, the Southern Kingdom, a shepherd, and a dresser of figs, Amos was commissioned by God to take His message of judgment to Israel, the Northern Kingdom. From all outward signs, Israel was prospering (a sure sign of God's pleasure?), but inwardly, the nation was a mass of spiritual corruption which had revealed itself in a whole series of social sins.

Before zeroing in on the sins of Israel, Amos classified the sins of its neighbors and announced God's coming judgment (1:3—2:5). The Syrians had been guilty of cruel brutality when they drove studded threshing-sleds over the bodies of their captives. The Philistines sold their fellow men into slavery. The people of Tyre and Edom had ignored the bonds of human kinship; and the Ammonites had committed atrocities to enlarge their borders. The Moabites had desecrated the corpse of a rival king, an act with social implications. Only Judah was cited for "religious" sins. The rest of Israel's neighbors were condemned for sins against humanity.

God had the same complaints about Israel. The nation's economy had been booming, but its wealth had become increasingly concentrated among the merchants who showed little concern for the growing needs of the peasants who at one time had been the backbone of Israel's society.

The newly prosperous merchants spent all their time improving their own living standards at the expense of others (3:10, 12, 15; 6:4). The signs were everywhere. The rich oppressed the poor (2:6–7), and the comfortable were heartlessly indifferent toward the afflictions of the hungry (6:3–6). In the courts there was an obvious double standard for the rich and the poor, and "justice" always went to the highest bidder (2:6; 8:6). While the merchants lived in the lap of luxury, the peasants (who were dependent on the land for their sustenance) suffered through drought and were forced to resort to moneylenders who demanded their land and even their persons as collateral (4:7–9; 5:11; 8:4–6).

Obviously, God took such social sins very seriously. They reflected a deep moral and spiritual crisis which had expressed itself in religious as well as social hypocrisy. The tragic thing about this situation was that the people were going through their normal religious practices as though everything was as it should be. Religion was not neglected; the people were faithful in their pious observances (5:5; 4:4–5). But it was being perverted by those people who erroneously believed that God would accept their worship while they were mistreating their fellow citizens (5:21–23).

From God's perspective, it is impossible to separate personal, religious, or social sins. They all stem from the same self-centeredness and alienation from God. God's righteous anger was aroused in each case. Whether the poor were oppressed, sexual license practiced (2:7), or religious ritual defiled, the result was the same—divine judgment.

God never told His prophets to avoid social questions. He did not instruct them to concentrate on the sins of the flesh or deviations from orthodox doctrine. Any offense to the righteousness of God was fair game. And any attempt to divide human life into neat categories such as public/private or personal/social was soundly rejected.

A Lopsided Gospel?

Why have we missed so obvious a message? Anyone who even superficially reads the Bible can readily see that God cares about *all* of life and expects His people to do the same.

Clearly, premillennialism can't carry the full blame for American evangelicalism's neglect of social righteousness. The issue is much larger than that.

Probably the major reason most evangelicals shy away from addressing the leading social problems of the day is that they believe that we must choose either between a social gospel which is primarily concerned with the transformation of society and an evangelistic gospel which chiefly concentrates on the salvation of souls. This idea has been so embedded in our evangelical churches for so long that many Christians are surprised (if not shocked) to learn that not too long ago evangelicals in America were convinced that the two could—and had to—go together!

It is impossible to get a true picture of evangelicalism without knowing something about the history of the American churches in the 19th century. As we noted in the last chapter, evangelicals in the previous century maintained a strong revivalistic emphasis *and* a commitment to social involvement and concern—with no apparent conflict of purpose or compromise in devotion to Christ.

A number of historical studies have attempted to trace this dual emphasis. Timothy Smith's *Revivalism and Social Reform: American Protestantism on the Eve of the Civil War* (New York: Harper and Row Publications, Inc., 1957) showed the close relationship between American revivalism and the attempts to reform and improve society before the Civil War. He demonstrated that revivalistic religion provided the founders, supporters, and much of the dedicated enthusiasm for the reforming societies. In the 19th century, American evangelicals believed that devotion to Jesus Christ as Saviour and Lord compelled them to be concerned about the world for which He died—and that included all aspects of society.

A similar book is Donald Dayton's *Discovering an Evangelical Heritage* (New York: Harper and Row Publications, Inc. 1976). Professor Dayton does a commendable job of showing how evangelicals in the last century were in the forefront of American reform movements. Jonathan Blanchard, the founder of Wheaton (Ill.) College, was considered a political radical by his contemporaries because he became a leader in the abolitionist movement to free the slaves (he was a civil rights worker) and even defied the law of the land by hiding fugitive slaves in the basement of a Wheaton College building!

Charles Finney believed that social reform was a natural outgrowth of conversion to Christ. Many of his converts devoted themselves to reform activities, and Finney himself played a major role in the founding of Oberlin College, an evangelical institution which was dedicated to breaking down all unchristian social barriers, including discrimination against blacks in society.

Other evangelicals threw themselves into the early feminist movement (which in its beginnings had obvious Christian ties), or sought ways to meet the needs of the poor and disadvantaged in the cities.

There was never total agreement in evangelicalism on

strategy or particular causes, but the overwhelming majority of evangelicals in the last century rarely doubted the propriety or advisability of trying to make things better. Belief in Christ as Saviour and Lord naturally led to that kind of social commitment.

But something happened toward the end of the century. People began to feel they had to choose between saving souls and transforming the social order. Why did this occur?

Most of the blame probably belongs to the rise of liberal theology. Unwilling to accept many of evangelicalism's fundamental doctrines (such as the deity of Christ, the Virgin Birth, the resurrection of Jesus, or even the need for salvation), the only thing many liberals felt comfortable doing was social work. They began to criticize those who spent time evangelizing. More could be accomplished by working to change social institutions. Thus the social gospel movement was born.

Let's get one thing clear. Not all "social gospelers" were theological liberals. Many of the founders of the movement testified to evangelical, personal conversions to Jesus Christ and stressed that conversion to Jesus was an absolute necessity. In time, however, they were outnumbered by liberals who cared very little for evangelism.

Naturally, when this occurred, other evangelicals began to steer clear of the social gospel movement. And many overreacted, claiming that the church's *only* task was saving souls. The end result was a polarization within the churches and the development of the idea that one had to choose between evangelism and social concern.

For decades now, that false concept has remained. In the fundamentalist movement anyone who showed the slightest concern for the "social" gospel was automatically branded a theological liberal and banished to the nether regions! Naturally, few people even discussed the possibility of trying to restore a more balanced and biblical approach to the Christian life.

The obvious tragedy of this polarization was that a basic truth of the Christian Gospel was nearly lost: one who has been redeemed by Jesus Christ will naturally come to share the Father's concern for social righteousness (remember Amos). As a result, for almost a century we have been producing Christians who are either afraid to become involved in the physical or social needs of the world, or who are simply unconcerned about them. Either position is a distortion of the Gospel and an affront to the loving concern of our Lord and Saviour.

Can a Premillennialist Be Socially Concerned?

Many of the evangelicals who are rediscovering this natural relationship between conversion to Christ and concern for the needs of the world are premillennialists who still are bothered by the relationship between their eschatology and social involvement. Can a premillennialist who is convinced that only the Second Coming will bring in a true social righteousness on a universal scale, still seek to correct and improve unrighteous social relationships and problems?

That's a good question. It's interesting to note that many of the people who became premillennialists at the end of the last century maintained the social commitment they had while they were postmillennialists!

Of course, their perspective had changed a bit. They no longer believed that social reform effort would bring in the Millennium. They now understood that the solution to man's basic social problems would come from beyond history through the Second Coming. Neither did they believe (if they ever did) that social action was on an equal par with evangelism. Concern for social righteousness does not vie with evangelism, but is a natural consequence of it.

The relationship between evangelism and social concern is similar to that between faith and works. One naturally flows out of the other. "What good is it, my brothers, if a man claims to have faith but has no deeds? Can such a faith save him? Suppose a brother or sister is without clothes and daily food. If one of you says to him, 'Go, I wish you well; keep warm and well fed,' but does nothing about his physical needs, what good is it? In the same way, faith by itself, if it is not accompanied by action, is dead" (James 2:14–17).

In a similar way, evangelism that is not accompanied by a concern for the whole person's needs is shallow and less than it should be.

What hadn't changed, when these former postmillennial believers became premillennialists, was their firm conviction that God was a righteous God who cared about all of life. The same God who judged Israel and its neighbors for social unrighteousness is still the Lord of the church. His concern hasn't changed. He still hates oppression of the poor, brutality, and the like as much as He ever did. And just because the final victory over Satan will not be won until Jesus' return doesn't mean that God's people are supposed to sit on their hands while Satan rages through the present age.

Christians, of all people, don't have to take that lying down. We are children of the kingdom, empowered by the Spirit, and adopted into God's own family. We have been equipped with God's armor to do battle against Satan. Are we supposed to get dressed in our armor and then hide in the closet until the last trumpet? Hardly. God equips us for conflict against Satan and all his wiles.

The church does not expect to conquer the world before the Second Coming, but it should recognize its call to be its salt and light until Jesus comes. As one early premillennialist in America said, just "because our politics or 'citizenship' is in heaven is no reason why we should let the rogues in some city hall steal our money, or the rumseller or the procurer debauch our youth. It is admitted that we are not undoing the works of Satan very fast, but we are giving him all the trouble we can till Jesus comes, and that is something."

Of all people, premillennialists should be speaking out against such things as social injustice, racial inequality, and unequal opportunity. We know that God hates such behavior and will shortly return to judge it. It is our obligation as Christ's ambassadors to inform those who perpetuate such evil that the King is coming to hold them to account. We know what will happen in the future; we are assured of sharing in the victory. Why not then anticipate that future triumph by speaking out here and now on those issues we know are close to the heart of God?

Our study has now ended, but God's work in the world has not. He has informed us of His future plans so that our lives might be transformed and enriched in the present. Let us take what we have learned about our Lord's coming, the establishment of His kingdom, and His final victory over all evil as a rallying point for deeper Christian discipleship. Our futures are secure in God. We have nothing to fear. God is in control and His purposes will be fulfilled.

"Do not be afraid, little flock, for your Father has been pleased to give you the kingdom. Sell your possessions and give to the poor. Provide purses for yourselves that will not wear out, a treasure in heaven that will not be exhausted, where no thief comes near and no moth destroys. For where your treasure is, there your heart will be also" (Luke 12:32–34).

For Further Reading

1. General

Millard J. Erickson, *Contemporary Options in Eschatology* (Grand Rapids: Baker Book House, 1977).

R. Ludwigson, *A Survey of Bible Prophecy* (Grand Rapids: Zondervan, 1975).

Robert G. Clouse, ed. *The Meaning of the Millennium: Four Views* (Downers Grove, Ill.: InterVarsity Press, 1977).

2. Pretribulational Premillennialism

Hal Lindsey, *The Late Great Planet Earth* (Grand Rapids: Zondervan, 1970).

Charles C. Ryrie, *Dispensationalism Today* (Chicago: Moody Press, 1965).

John F. Walvoord, *The Rapture Question* (Findlay, O.: Dunham, 1957).

John F. Walvoord, *The Return of the Lord* (Findlay, O.: Dunham, 1955).

3. Posttribulational Premillennialism

Robert H. Gundry, *The Church and the Tribulation* (Grand Rapids: Zondervan, 1973).

George E. Ladd, *The Blessed Hope* (Grand Rapids: Eerdmans, 1956).

George E. Ladd, *The Last Things* (Grand Rapids: Eerdmans, 1978).

Arthur Katterjohn, *The Tribulation People* (Carol Stream, Ill.: Creation House, 1975).